Under Fire

Under Fire

Reporting from the Front Lines of the Trump White House

April Ryan

ROWMAN & LITTLEFIELD
Lanham • Boulder • New York • London

Published by Rowman & Littlefield
An imprint of The Rowman & Littlefield Publishing Group, Inc.
4501 Forbes Boulevard, Suite 200, Lanham, Maryland 20706
www.rowman.com

Unit A, Whitacre Mews, 26-34 Stannary Street, London SE11 4AB

Distributed by NATIONAL BOOK NETWORK

British Library Cataloguing in Publication Information Available

Library of Congress Cataloging-in-Publication Data

978-1-5381-1336-3 (cloth)
978-1-5381-1337-0 (electronic)

♾ ™ The paper used in this publication meets the minimum requirements of American National Standard for Information Sciences—Permanence of Paper for Printed Library Materials, ANSI/NISO Z39.48-1992.

Printed in the United States of America

Contents

Foreword

By Tamron Hall

*T*hey say April showers bring May flowers.

For two decades April has journeyed the road that makes one a great journalist while juggling the job of mother, author, and advocate. The day she went "viral" with the head-shake heard 'round cable news, social media, and eventually global news was just one of April's defining moments. The heated exchange defined her spirit, but not her struggle and her gracious tenacity that not only got her to the dance, but kept her feet moving no matter what was thrown her way. In this memoir, April connects the dots missing from the viral moment. How did the reporter, focused on urban world issues, take the conversation beyond race and put it smack on the doorstep of all watching, and her many now famous moments after? This mother, who balanced work and tears after feeling under siege by some of her own colleagues, managed to get up every single time. What her supporters love most about April, and trust me there are many from all walks of life, is her ability to keep her eye on what matters.

I don't believe for a second that the viral moment that comes up when you search her name defines this woman. It actually should make you want to learn how she got in that hot seat without letting it burn her. How she knew when to nod and when to go in for the question.

April's approach to one of the most intimidating jobs in journalism has not changed from administration to administration. While the players and faces shift, her perspective is cemented in the responsibility of the position as a woman, and most importantly, as a Black woman. This has led to numerous awards and praise from the most unlikely places. But as she details, for every moment of praise there was the gut punch of life so many face. No time to glance twice at the National Association of Black Journalists award because looking down too long would only distract from the mission at hand, the mission of reporting the facts and making sure the urban audience counting on her to ask that race question would not be ignored or marginalized.

April has kept that girlfriend quality with the hard and highly praised skill set of a Cronkite or Murrow. She was not formed in their image, but one of her own with the same dedication to the people who count on her. The people who watched her not knowing this unprecedented place she would end up in that day when the head shook and soil broke free for April to rise.

It's never about her, but when you have worked this hard and been discounted by even the most progressive in the room, you become okay with leaning in, around, and ultimately not backing down.

I love that April is not afraid of the showers no matter how hard the rain pours down. I could end on a cliché about the sun emerging to dry her tears and free her from worry, but that would be a fairy tale and nothing about her journey lends itself to such predictable or average endings.

Tamron Hall
Broadcast journalist and television host

Acknowledgments

Thank you, God, for this incredible journey! I could never have dreamed what you have placed before me.

Mommy and Daddy, all I ever wanted was to make you proud of me. I hope you are, and I love you both so much! Mommy, I hope you receive that in heaven, and Daddy, I hope you feel that here on Earth.

Ryan and Grace. I love you to life! You two are my everything.

To my brother, Robert, thanks for always wanting me to go higher and offering ideas. Keep sending them.

To Ella, thanks for having that sparkle in your eyes about Aunt April.

Diane Nine, thank you for pushing me and making my book dreams come true.

Dave Smitherman, thank you for always being part of the team and for being a great sounding board and editor.

Audia and David, thank you for never letting me give up and telling me the magic is there. You have lifted my spirit in good times and bad. Thank you for your friendship.

To my family, thanks for the prayers and support.

To Baltimore and the Morgan State University community, thank you for the love.

To my close circle of friends and all of you who listened to me and cried with me over past last year, thank you!!!!

To everyone who offered your voice in this book, thank you! Your voices are needed for a time such as this!

To my publisher, thank you for allowing me to have another opportunity to tell my story and do it my way! Jon and the Rowman & Littlefield crew, thank you.

To American Urban Radio Networks, thank you for giving me this platform for the past twenty-one years.

To CNN, thank you for a great year. I am so grateful to be able to work with such amazing people who work so hard to get the stories right!!! No fake news here!

To Lafayette 148, thank you for inspiring me through fashion over the many years. I adore all of you! Much love!

To the National Association of Black Journalists, thank you for acknowledging me in 2017. You have been the wind beneath my wings during this crazy, yet amazing, year.

To all my "ride or die" fans, thank you for the support on the street, on social media, and anywhere you show your love. I feel it! It has been one of the factors that has sustained me over this tough period of time. On the darkest days, you find ways to pick me up, and for that I am thankful.

As I always say, don't hug me when you see me. Pray for me.

Be blessed and enjoy the pages.

Introduction

These pages are meant to shed a bright light in the dark spaces. These dark spaces are the stories I cover daily and the people who have been an integral part of my beat since the 2016 election cycle. This book is born out of the new era that we are now in, an era of divisiveness in which racism is on the rise, our nation's values of democracy are in peril, truth is not respected, and a free and independent press is under siege. In this era, a president is called "racist," a president who has used discriminatory words and failed to implement an agenda that will improve the lives of disenfranchised Black and Brown residents of our cities. After a year in office, the only Black agenda item this president can tout is the decline in the Black unemployment numbers, which are lower than ever. But the devil is in the details. Black unemployment continues, as in the past, to be almost two times that of White America, with teen unemployment the highest. This is nothing new.

I have worked my beat at the White House for twenty-one years, and I have never seen anything like the turmoil, the social and political polarization, the federal investigations, and the attacks on the press. Nothing compares. Nothing! Mind you, I was a kid when the Nixon and Watergate scandals swirled, but from what I am told and from what I remember, the current situation tops even that. I remember everyone back then being riveted, wondering about what could be next. The same thing is happening now. It's eerie. Yet the gravity of the current situation is beyond all that. It is beyond the Russian investigation; it is beyond the Black and Brown agenda. It is even beyond domestic violence and security clearance. What this administration has done is to scare Americans and the global communities about the fragility of democracies. All this because of one person—Donald J. Trump.

It is about the reckless disregard for the truth and the ever-so-dangerous fight against an independent and free press. This matchup of an American president against a free press could change the dynamic for the worse for years down the road. A press will win only by reporting and uncovering the truth, even if that truth is hard to swallow. We cannot fight back any other way. This year of history has poisoned the ink-well against the press, singling out those who ask questions that some feel challenge the president and/or his system of governing.

As a member of the White House press corps, I have a unique perch to witness history, which I have been doing for more than two decades. I say that with pride. Not everyone can say that; I am one of the few folks who can. I have garnered the right to compare and contrast after witnessing four American presidents come and go even as I stay.

The unrelenting chaos that characterizes the Trump presidency and the administration's gleeful disregard for the truth is unprecedented. Will it challenge our democracy? At President Trump's first solo press conference, in February 2017, he regaled us about how his administration was a "fine-tuned machine." Well, the machine is out of tune. Some wonder if this administration will explode or implode. Will its fuse continue to burn until it's too late? Or will it be defused? Stay tuned as we all watch it unfold, for better or worse. One thing is for sure: We have never seen anything like this before!

When it comes to reporting on matters of race, the old haunts of the past are back with a new and emboldened, at times angrier, face on them. The time is here when the influencers in this White House think they can do a sleight of hand and people will not see what is really happening. The pages of this book further remove the veil of mystery from the workings of the White House, particularly the Trump administration with its unique approach to handling the mainstream press. Depending on which portion of the political spectrum you stand is where your thoughts are on all of this. I can't speak for what you feel, but I can tell you what I see. And that is fact. There is nothing "fake" here.

I would like to say that when the word *fake* is hurled at members of the press, it makes my skin crawl. What would happen if we did a word swap and started calling the president *fake*? Most people cannot handle it when the demeaning words they dish out are flipped and used on them. Seriously, how would President Trump react? Knowing how he has reacted during the past two years he has been in the political limelight, it would not be pretty. It would for sure create an unpleasant atmosphere of hate. That is what we do not want!

However, something else that none of us want is happening to the press now. The hate is oozing onto us, but people often forget that we are people too. We go to our houses of worship and to the grocery store. We coach little league baseball. We are contributing members of society. People forget that we are your relatives, neighbors, and friends. We just happen to be in this time-tested, constitutionally supported, honorable profession of journalism. We have not committed a crime so we shouldn't be treated like criminals, even though the Trump White House wants punishment leveled against us for telling the truth. What time period are we talking about? What country in the free world does that? Not the greatest country in the world, the United States of America. Until now. Europe is watching us in fear as we embark on this new journey of an American presidential experiment against the press and in which high standards of presidential conduct are brought low.

As a reporter, I am supposed to get all sides of the story, never inter-jecting myself. This year I have been a walking contradiction to that theory. I never intended for all this to happen. But along the way in my reporting, I have been lied about, and talked about—all with an effort to discredit me. Unfortunately, I *have* become the story. I have been unwillingly pulled into the story, a part of the history of this magnificent place, the White House. Many of us in the press have been singled out, sometimes subtly and other times with blatant and public accusations.

Since that happened to me, since I became part of the story, I have been harshly criticized by some and applauded by others. I find it most interesting that some do not understand why I ask the questions I do. Often these days, people react first before understanding what they are talking about. I have often been called a "race baiter." Of course, it's just the opposite. I bring up questions related to race to inform the pub-lic so that things can improve, not worsen. I'm not a race baiter, but I hope to be a *race informer.* Those who make such an unfounded accusa-tion need to do their research and understand the complicated history of race in this country before slinging that ugly term.

In this book, you will walk with me and learn the backstory of some of the major news events of 2017 and early 2018. Truth is the important aspect of my job, especially now. Truth is verifiable. There is no spin or talking points in this book—just the facts. This is my side of the story as I have lived it. I will take you on my daily journey to report the news. Along the way, I have made new friendships and severed toxic ones. Sadly, most were cut from my life because of the new political climate and the novice breed of politicians that has entered the established Washington, D.C., landscape.

By the way, because the stakes are so high, I have validation for what I report in this book. I have various on-the-record interviews with people who can support the claims contained within.

It astonishes me when people ask me how I keep going back every day to report the truth despite the condescension, name calling, threats, and other abuse. Initially, I was shocked to get that question, but then I realized that they see what I have to endure and are legitimately concerned when I put myself in a situation of vulnerability. But I have the first amendment of the Constitution to back me up. So, I press on.

First, I have done nothing wrong. I am doing my job, and it's a job I love. Second, I fall back on a phrase my mother would quote of Dr. King, who said, "It is not what they call you but what you answer to." Third, I am that kid who was told to dream when folks threw darts at my ideas. I was told as a child to set my goals high and work hard and get a good education to obtain whatever I imagined. I did what my parents told me and am now fulfilling my destiny. I am the young child who read Maya Angelou's poetry collection *And Still I Rise*. I understood the meaning, which allowed me to rise daily for the challenge. One portion of the poem resounds as clear to me as the clang of the Liberty Bell that I had the opportunity to ring in 2016. I hold dear the portion of her poem that says, *You may write me down in history / With your bitter, twisted lies / You may trod me in the very dirt / But still, like dust, I'll rise.*

I was also the young child who listened to the dreamer who talked of a day when there would be racial equality. Personally, I am still holding on to that dream and am in search of the promise this county has yet to fully offer. So, with that, I will not be daunted, and I will not bow down or bow out. I rise to meet the workday and its challenges at 1600 Pennsylvania Avenue, and I do it with an eager pride. As the late Shirley Chisholm said, "If they don't give you a seat at the table, bring a folding chair." Well, in my case, I am bringing a pen and a pad and a digital recorder.

I hope this book causes you to think critically about the condition of our country and of the press. The chapters in these pages will help you to see the challenges for what they are. I hope as you read you are compelled to push for a better day, as I am. This book is not meant to be vicious toward anyone or any group, and the tone is not meant to be bitter, but it is meant to be blunt. I am setting the record straight with truth and facts, and with figures if need be. My hope always is to aspire to inspire.

Sit back and just read. Some of this is quite amazing and astonishing.

· 1 ·

The Rebuke

"*If* you don't like something, change it. If you can't change it, change your attitude." Those words by Maya Angelou accurately summarize the political landscape in 2017. People are usually resistant to change, but not this time. The result of the 2016 presidential election wasn't simply about a change from the previous administration and its policies. It was a complete rebuke of the previous eight years of the Obama administration. The rebuke is where my story begins.

On January 20, 2017, at 12:01 p.m., the nation embarked on its latest untested experiment: a businessman with no governance experience assumed the highest office in the land, president of the United States of America. On the surface, people wanted something new, but what was the definition of new? What I discovered was that they did not know!

Both parties, Democrats and Republicans, and those on the fringes wanted a fresh face on old issues. They wanted "change." That word had resounded in at least two of the most recent presidential elections. The hope for the next president was someone with new ideas, a new way to take on the established political process, a person with a creative approach to breaking the same old political cycle that left so many feeling that government was not serving them. In the minds of the Washington GOP establishment, better yet, the government elite, the election of Donald Trump was a bold move meant to quell the unending hunger to break the system. The nation's appetite for change was palpable. From the onset, however, the GOP never welcomed the bombastic, at times sophomoric, business mogul who had captured the attention of the "forgotten man"—young, white, rural Americans, pre-

7

dominantly males, typically without a college degree. That sounds so harsh, but it is so true. That demographic, that portion of America that had decided they had been overlooked during the Obama years, was the target for Trump's unconventional campaign. The strategy worked, and Trump's campaign hit a bullseye.

The Washington, D.C., establishment never embraced fully Donald Trump, not before the primaries and not even after the general election; they still haven't. One of the main reasons for Trump's inability to assimilate with most politicians is his inability to take the spotlight off himself and shine it on the country as he should be doing. For example, on October 25, 2017, Trump headed for Dallas to assess federal efforts after Hurricane Harvey. Before boarding the plane, he talked to some members of the White House press corps. He proclaimed that he had attended an "Ivy League school" (Wharton). He also asserted that he is "intelligent." Even though Trump was headed on a serious mission where people had lost their lives and livelihoods, he felt compelled to talk about himself.

Despite his business acumen and his education, Trump continues to come across as a bombastic, brash outsider on the fringe, not a "true Republican." His brashness and the crude language and his simple sentences are how he had connected with the "forgotten man"; that's what they responded to. Trump supporters claimed that he was just like them. Somehow, this rich New York real estate tycoon seemed relatable to them, even though his life had been far from anything most of them ever experienced. Possibly because Trump's challenger was a Democrat and for the first time a woman who actually had a chance to win, his supporters were able to push all the negative aspects of their candidate aside. For these rural supporters, the closest they could likely ever come to the Trump lifestyle was by chanting their support in front of one of his hotels, unable to afford the overpriced rooms inside.

Many don't want to remember the truth, but Trump was once a registered Democrat who financially supported other Democrats during his early years in New York. How do I know? I saw it for myself. I was in New York in a beautifully decorated apartment in Trump Tower at a fundraiser for a then-Democratic New York congressman, my cousin Ed Towns. Not only was I in attendance for that event, but so was then-president Bill Clinton, who was hemmed in by Trump the entire evening. Those who had gathered and had financially supported my cousin waited and waited in line for pictures to be taken with their hero—and their hero wasn't Trump, it was Bill Clinton.

Trump couldn't or wouldn't pull himself away from the charismatic ex-president. Trump continued with his long-winded conversation, oblivious to the line that had formed and the protests of others for him to wrap it up. They did not appreciate someone monopolizing Clinton's time, even if that person was millionaire Donald Trump.

In full disclosure, even though I was Ed Towns's cousin (a blood relative on my mother's side), I did not that night (nor any other) donate to a political campaign. Yes, I love my cousin, but he understood my position. I was there to support him with my presence and see how these sorts of fundraisers work, especially in the world of high-profile politicians. It just so happened that at the fundraiser in that lush apartment of a woman native to my family's home community in North Carolina, I got my first up-close glimpse of Donald Trump, the man who would switch his allegiance to another political party and run for president years later . . . and win. That night was also my initial insight into Mr. Trump. I reached out to shake his hand and he basically blew me off as no big deal. He had his sights set on something bigger—Bill Clinton.

I would have never imagined, after watching Trump monopolize Bill Clinton's time, that he would later run against Hillary Clinton and paint her to be evil and dishonest. When I saw him, he seemed to have no problem with the Clintons. From what I now know of him, he was likely excited to be near someone so powerful. His motives may have been related to his businesses, or he might have just wanted to be associated with someone more powerful and influential than himself. It was an interesting night, and I couldn't believe someone supposedly so successful was conducting himself like that in public. It was an eerie foreshadowing of what has now come to fruition.

Meanwhile, returning to the 2016 election cycle, the rift was evident between this unconventional candidate and the Republican National Committee (RNC). What was most telling was that the RNC's typical election push for their presidential nominee did not mirror the efforts of years past. It was toned down, less . . . vocal, because of the rift between the establishment Republican Party operatives and the Trump campaign. My Republican sources involved in the RNC process contend that the RNC would normally have sent about 80 percent of its staff and funding to the Republican presidential nominee, but that did not happen during the 2016 election cycle. The RNC sent only about 20 percent of its financial support to the Trump camp when he was the presumed nominee for the party. The rift was evident with the whispers of dissension bubbling to the surface and going beyond the walls of the RNC and out into the community. It was very clear that the RNC's support for Trump was measured.

The RNC's approach to the 2016 election differed in another way. Early on, the RNC was strategic in its effort to court the Black vote. It had crunched the numbers and believed that a Republican candidate could not win the election without the minority vote. And so, the organization invited Black journalists to RNC headquarters as part of its game plan for winning the election. Laying out a strategy for winning a presidential election was not a new concept, nothing we hadn't heard before. What was key was the outreach to us, as representatives of the Black community and our chance to be part of that RNC connection. The inclusion of Black reporters was meant to have a two-fold benefit. The RNC wanted their candidates' stories aired, published, and hopefully televised in the Black community. We, the Black journalists, wanted something too. We wanted connections to the candidates so we could underpin our on-the-record stories with supporting quotes. We wanted in on the potpourri of candidates that season, which included Ted Cruz, Jeb Bush, Carly Fiorina, Ben Carson, Rand Paul, John Kasich, Chris Christie, and Donald Trump. You may not be aware that as Black journalists and the Black media, we are often not given access to Republican candidates. Our community is usually written off because it's not considered worthwhile to court our vote. So, it was an important moment for us during this historic election filled with a crowded field of candidates.

To be honest, there were so many candidates at first that it was confusing trying to keep up with which one supported which policies. Despite what others may think, the Black media wants to cover every angle of a story, even if the Black community as a whole may or may not agree with a policy personally. This is our job, and we want to present all sides of the story, with quotes from both parties, Democrats and Republicans.

I recall this RNC meeting very well, the one and only meeting I attended during the 2016 presidential run at the RNC headquarters, which is near the Capitol building. The weather was cold, and I was rushing to get there. I hurried into the building and then hung my heavy dress coat up on the rack. It felt like maybe I was wasting time as everyone was already in the room talking, meeting, and greeting. But then I realized I was not late at all. The room was filled with many Black journalists; some I knew and some I was not so familiar with. That was the evening I formally met Yamiche Alcindor, then of *The New York Times*. Also in attendance was Wes Lowery, author and reporter for *The Washington Post*, and multimedia reporter Lauren Victoria Burke. My invite had come via my work relationship with Telly Lovelace, who used to work at the RNC. Lovelace was once head of Black outreach in the communications shop under Sean Spicer, who was then RNC strategist and press secretary.

At the time of this RNC meeting with Black journalists, the organization was led by Reince Priebus, flanked by Sean Spicer. With this meeting, they were ready to kick off their initiative to embrace the Black community by first providing something we had usually been denied—access. Priebus and Spicer came across as the dynamic duo of Republican king makers this go around. I'm not sure who was Batman and who was Robin. They were leaning against the wall in the conference room as if they had all the confidence in the world, like this was a win on many levels.

They introduced some of the Black power brokers in the RNC and allowed them to talk. One of those was senior advisor to the chairman, Elroy Sailor. We listened and were ready with questions. Priebus and Spicer said they "needed" us. They needed a working relationship with us. They began to peel back the onion, even presenting charts on the dry-erase board to show how minorities have factored into the past presidential election cycles on both sides of the aisle.

I appreciated their presentation, but I was not sure why they felt the need to tell us about the power of the minority vote. We were well aware of our impact. (This is something that was demonstrated later when Roy Moore lost his bid for Alabama senator due in large part to the Black vote, particularly Black women. Alabama's Black Belt, which refers to the region's rich black soil, put Doug Jones over the top for the win.)

Back at the RNC, the dynamic duo made it abundantly clear that Black voters would have a major role in helping to elect the next Grand

Old Party president in 2016, even as the party's splinters were already beginning to be apparent as the candidates struggled to be heard. The Republican Party was also dividing into groups: conservative, religious right, neocons, Tea Party, Libertarians, far right, and evangelicals. With all those divisions, where would Black America fit?

After listening to their presentations, I was still trying to determine how genuine they were. I have seen many politicians work for the vote and heard endless promises and deals being made. I have become good at being able to tell when one part is saying whatever they have to in order to get what they want. Believe me, many people will do whatever it takes to get their way in Washington. As I watched the Priebus and Spicer show, I studied them to determine their angle, yet I was confused. They were obviously rehearsed, which isn't necessarily a bad thing, and they did come across as sincere.

So, I did what I always do when I need more information. I asked a question. "How do you plan to get your lead candidate, Donald Trump, to conform to this reach for Black and Brown America when his rhetoric is so divisive?" I knew everyone in the room was probably thinking the same thing, so that's why I asked. Often, I use that as my barometer when deciding if I should ask a question at a particular time. Getting an answer depends on many variables. Finding the perfect scenario is not easy, but it can be rewarding when it works out. So, after I asked my question, the duo said that it would be "easy" to convince their candidate that the Black vote is an important one. Trump would need the "data" they had already compiled, and they said they would present it when and if he moved on in the general election cycle; that is, if Trump complied with or fell in line with the RNC. They had it all planned out.

Thinking back on how Priebus and Spicer felt they could control Donald Trump makes me shake my head in disbelief. (Yes, I said, "shake my head"!) It amazes me that they had no clear understanding of how wrong they were, of what they were up against. Their calculations were totally off. Candidate Donald Trump did not want or need the Black and Brown votes as originally expressed by the RNC. Did Trump even want Black outreach before he realized who his core audience would be? Or was this specific White fringe base always his target audience?

Trump knew he was not going after the traditional Republican voter. He needed to tap into that group that felt hurt and excluded from the previous eight years of government. He also had to expand that umbrella even more to include the racially biased, aiming for those who not only disliked having a Democrat in the Oval Office for two terms but particularly a Black man. Trump tapped into the hate and disdain for inclusion and diversity; he embraced the rampant xenophobia. He tapped into the "forgotten man."

However, the split between the RNC and the Trump campaign was evident, and that split was a delicate situation, to say the least. In the last four to six months of campaigning, the RNC brought on a number of Black Republicans to help secure GOP wins because many of the Black staffers had left earlier in the year. Those staffers worked on congressional, state, and local races trying to get the Black vote out. The RNC's concern was that the Trump campaign would hurt turnout of traditional Black Republicans and independent Black voters.

So, there were two campaigns going on simultaneously. The Trump campaign did not court the Black establishment at all, and instead went for people like Sheriff David Clarke, Omarosa Manigault-Newman, YouTube personalities Diamond and Silk, Pastor Darrell Scott, Paris Dennard, and Bruce LeVell.

It was telling that none of the Blacks from the Trump campaign were at that RNC-Black reporter meeting. The Trump campaign never gave Black reporters the opportunity that the RNC had just offered. The RNC, with the approval of Reince Priebus, even went as far as to authorize the Black barbershop tour. The tour targeted barbershops in Republican districts as the focal point of the effort in Wisconsin, Georgia, Ohio, Michigan, Florida, and Virginia. In Virginia, even White congressional candidate Barbara Comstock ventured to a Black barbershop.

The Trump calculation was easy to figure out without any in-depth computation or strategist, but political scholar David Bositis offered these numbers days after the 2016 presidential election. In a November 13, 2016, email he wrote that the Black vote for Hillary Clinton was 88 percent, the same as for John Kerry in 2004. Trump received 8 percent of the Black vote. Black women voted overwhelmingly for Hillary Clinton by 94 percent verses Donald Trump at 4 percent.

A January 21, 2017, online *Vox* article read, "The Women Who Helped Donald Trump Win." The article notes, "Many women not only voted for him but were key in getting him over the top." Although 54 percent of women voted for Clinton compared with Trump's 42 percent, Trump did better among White women, receiving 53 percent.

Feminist and staunch women's rights advocate Gloria Steinem offered her thoughts on December 5, 2017, during a podcast interview for American Urban Radio Networks. She said Black women voted overwhelmingly for Hillary Clinton compared with "married White women who voted in the majority with 51 percent" for Donald Trump. Steinem profoundly added, "I don't mean to oversimplify, but they were probably voting for their husband's interests because they are dependent economically and socially on their husband's identity."

It is significant that unmarried White women did not vote in the majority for Trump and, of course, that more than 90 percent of Black women voted for Hillary Clinton. And Black women are more likely to be independent in their thought process and therefore they well understand what their own interests are.

The eighty-plus-year-old rights advocate believes it is a matter of consciousness: "It always makes me think of the great Harriet Tubman who said when she was praised for going into the dark of night in the South and helping to liberate hundreds and hundreds of slaves, 'I could have liberated many more if only they knew they were slaves.' We must always remember it is about consciousness. There is hope in the fact that at least 49 percent of [White married] women voted their own interests."

Digging further into the weeds of the statistics post the 2016 presidential election, Black men voted 80 percent for Hillary Clinton and 13 percent for Donald Trump. And 7 percent of the votes went to other candidates. The Pew Research Center also offers that Black voter turnout numbers were down for the first time in two decades, falling to 59.6 percent in 2016 after setting a record high in 2012 of 66.6 percent. Meanwhile, Pew says the Latino voter turnout rate was not enough for a win but held relatively steady for the past two elections at 47.6 percent in 2016, favoring Clinton compared with 48 percent in 2012. Summing it all up, fewer Blacks and Hispanics went to the polls, but more Whites voted, with a record 137.5 million people casting ballots in the 2016 election cycle. However, Bositis also said that "47 million working and lower-middle-class Whites didn't vote or voted for Democrats in opposition to Republican elites."

But what boggles my mind is that the Black and Brown communities in this country have the highest numbers of negatives in every category. So why is voter apathy in the Black and Brown communities creeping back into the discussion at a time when voter suppression is still an issue, more than fifty years after the Voting Rights Act was passed into law? I guess that is a question for another day. Yet, it is still a very real issue. And now we sit in a moment where we voted for the first time in fifty years without the full protections of the Voting Rights Act. Also, to be clear, I want people to vote, I don't care who for. Why? Too many people marched, had dogs bite their flesh, and had hoses turned on them with the burning sting of pressurized water on their skin. And some even died fighting for the vote. Not exercising that privilege means not honoring those sacrifices. I don't want to be on a soapbox, but it's very clear, especially for minorities, that voting is an important right and privilege that should be taken seriously. You are not sending a message of protest when you don't vote. You are compounding the problem and, in some cases, getting exactly what you did not want.

As some of the loud voices of the Republican and Washington establishment continued to rebuke Donald Trump during the campaign, he was politically cunning enough to confound the pollsters and beat the system, and he even challenged the traditions of his own party. Donald Trump, a political phenomenon with a provocative in-your-face approach, did gain popularity because of the support of those who wanted "change." However, how did he cross the finish line? How did he do it? The answer can be summed up in one word: race. It is a passionate issue for all sides on the spectrum. It is something we still can't all civilly agree on. For those who wanted to keep things the way they used to be, this was their brash candidate who proudly rejected political correctness and connected with those who felt they had been left behind.

In a November 13, 1988, *Washington Post* opinion piece titled "What a Real President Was Like," Bill Moyers noted that in 1960 in Tennessee after a meeting with local dignitaries, then-Vice President Lyndon Baines Johnson said something that rings so true this day: "If you can convince the lowest White man he's better than the best Colored man, he won't notice you're picking his pocket. Hell, give him somebody to look down on, and he'll empty his pockets for you."

Another tactic Trump used to galvanize his core supporters came to me in an "aha moment." In the summer of 2017, I took my kids to New York City to see the Broadway musical *Wicked* for the third time. Yet more importantly, to see actress Sheryl Lee Ralph who played Madame Morrible, the headmistress of the school. My friend made theater history by being the first Black woman to play Madame Morrible on Broadway.

It was art imitating life when one of the characters began to reveal the plot of the play making the green witch the enemy of Oz. The character said the best way to "unify" people is to create "a common enemy." Mind you, *Wicked* the book was published in 1995 and the play was a Broadway musical in 2003. This thought pattern was laid well before Donald Trump decided to create a common enemy, but he understood what to do.

Indeed, that is the formula in real life. The "enemy" (Barack Obama) became the 44th president of the United States. That strategy was crafted years ago when Trump raised the issue of Obama's legitimacy as president by questioning his birth country. Trump claimed that Obama had been born in Kenya, not in the United States, which would make Obama ineligible to be president. This falsehood, birtherism, spread like wildfire among those like-minded individuals. People found it so hard to believe that a world-traveled White woman from Kansas, who married a Black African man in Hawaii, could actually have a Black baby in the United States. Hawaii is part of the United States! (I have to add that because during Hurricane Maria, folks seemed to forget that Puerto Rico is a U.S. territory and that Puerto Ricans are U.S. citizens.)

But Trump's claim was never about the birth certificate. The issue was clearly race-based, and it was more about the pigment of the baby's skin and that of the baby's father as well. Father and baby were both guilty of being Black, which is still the unwritten crime this nation subtly acknowledges in everyday life. That fact is that Trump jumped on that bandwagon and continued his personal campaign to find the "real" birth certificate. Much like O. J. Simpson was going to find the "real" killer, Trump was supposedly hiring private investigators to locate the real birth certificate. That fact that Barack Obama eventually released a copy of his birth certificate did nothing to sway the naysayers, mainly because it was just the beginning of what is now commonplace. It was the start of this perception that you can make up anything to attack someone's credibility if you don't agree with them. No facts are needed because they only get in the way of the real mission, to tarnish someone's reputation.

The establishment that rebuked Trump and his political aspirations did not chastise his brash and seemingly racist push against Obama. It was the pay-off and the action that the presidential candidate craved and was diligent in creating. It ultimately built his brand for the White House years later. Even though the GOP turned a blind eye to the birther issue, Trump was still not warmly welcomed into the Republican Party by the establishment, nor was he considered an asset. He walked into the White House with this issue lingering overhead; the divide between the president and his party was palpable.

However, Trump's winning the presidential election is not only about race. Beyond the code words and dog whistles, there is a policy element. Donald Trump, as a Democrat turned Republican (DTR) candidate, eventually moved toward supporting many primary Republican policy issues that reflect the core of GOP: pro-life, pro-marriage, pro-gun (at that time), anti-tax, anti-climate change. Also, in a bold and ultimately successful move, candidate Trump played up "draining the swamp," which meant change for those who felt stuck. That word *change* was like water for the American thirst. That word was the hope and dream of a new day and had been the link for the presidential wins of Barack Obama eight years earlier. Donald Trump used the same "change" terminology, which demonstrates that it can mean anything to anyone. For Obama, it was hope and change. For Trump, it was just change, something different—something that was not Obama. Hope for certain segments of America never played into the equation, and now we know why.

For me, it was not a surprise that Donald Trump immediately followed Barack Obama as president. Congressional Black Caucus chair Cedric Richmond also understood the rise of a political Donald Trump and says it was constructed by "pandering to a base of Trump's that is not sensitive to minorities and others" and that is not focused on "equal rights and equal protections."

Richmond also says, "I think we are in that period of backlash after a large or huge African American gain. Throughout history, every time we have made significant gains, there has been a fierce and ferocious backlash from those who have resented it. Whether it was the end of reconstruction, whether it was Jim Crow or whether it was the Tea Party or Donald Trump movement against President Obama."

In this latest round of political fisticuffs, the dog whistle sounded, and people ran to Make America Great Again (MAGA), despite not having any frame of reference for what that would mean. My constant question is about the word *again* and the timeline for the greatest period in the nation's history. If my history is correct, at no time in this country's effort to be better than before has it ever witnessed all Americans sharing first-class citizenship. What is the timeline when America was great? With positives and negatives and its scars and keloids, America is great, but that doesn't change the fact that we must fix the issues that remain from the past.

Trump's MAGA calls pulled together a certain group that many in the Republican establishment did not identify with. Nonetheless, the party was forced to embrace its nominee even though he appeared to be under the impression that he was about to be crowned king. What was no longer subtle in this nation, especially after the last five decades, was an overt rebuke of the first Black president of the United States. It was more than just a notion or a thought. We could hear it at the water cooler at work, see it on the nightly news, and engage with it in almost every aspect of life. It was here again, the hate of the past masked with a new face, under a political guise. The rebuke of Barack Hussein Obama had arrived.

However, when Obama won the election the first time, the nation was struggling to pull itself out of a self-imposed recession caused by the eight previous years of little financial regulation and oversight and a costly war. Back then, Obama was hope and change; he was the one who was going to save us. As promised, under his administration, the economy stabilized, and the nation was gaining momentum in seeing its best self. It was not about politics or policy but a matter of getting the country back on track. The job was left to a Black man, and he was ultimately successful. However, many seemed to find difficulty in giving him credit. Although a Black man had helped to right the tilted economy, he was still guilty of being a Black man in the highest office in the land.

Even though he didn't always get his due, there was more focus on racial equality and diversity. Make no mistake, there were people of all races and backgrounds who welcomed the shift in this nation and applauded the tear in its flawed fabric that sometimes embraces hate and injustice. It was more than patriotic to see the nation rise to its best self and complete the call for true equality that not even the Constitution had written on its pages. "All men are created equal." In a society of all types of people—be it gender, race, sexual orientation, or religion—we have never fully seen the equality of all people. However, something no one ever expected finally happened! A Black man as president of the United States.

Naturally, that was a big change from the previous administration, and there were some in various sectors who did not like it at all. Even some who were well meaning did not, or could not, accept the fact that a Black man achieved the highest, most prestigious, and powerful office in the land. In 2008, forty-seven-year-old Barack Obama handily defeated his Republican challenger, Senator John McCain. Even Senator McCain had to defend then-candidate Obama from a White woman who called him Muslim. We had no idea what would come years later.

One of the fantastic nuances is that the same Black man more than 150 years ago could have been a slave in this country, but now he was the leader living in a home built by slaves. That feat alone should have been celebrated by every American; it was the ultimate American success story! There was no question of the popular vote or the electoral college victory. Barack Hussein Obama was the 44th president of the United States. Now a bit of pigment splashed the pictures of the lineage of the nation's presidents. However, eight years to the day, the shift happened—change from a lawyer/politician to a businessman/politician.

New Orleans congressman Cedric Richmond conveyed that America knew Donald Trump as a "corporate executive" with "bad business practices." The congressman said that at first blush you'd never view Donald Trump as a "citizen with community focus. So, you always thought of him as being Donald Trump. There is no adjective for him. He is his own adjective."

Decades ago, Donald Trump drew acclaim and attention for his real estate and entertainment prowess, and simultaneously he was teased about the possibility of a run for president. His comments were always newsworthy, which worked out well for him because he liked staying in the news. It is not shocking that he publicly supported Democratic politicians on his Republican ascent to power, not knowing he would gain the Oval Office in 2017, immediately following the first Black president. Trump began to pull large numbers of people into his ill-informed rhetoric with the claim that President Barack Obama was not a legitimate president because he had been born in Africa. Some people listened because that's what they wanted to hear. Trump learned a lot during the birther movement.

When it comes to perceived racial insensitivity issues, Trump has consistently raised eyebrows over the decades. Trump was on record calling for the death penalty with his thoughts about the 1989 Central Park Five attack on a White female jogger in which five males, Black and Hispanic, were charged and convicted of rape and served six and thirteen years in prison until a serial rapist confessed to the crime.

Then there was a huge housing discrimination issue. Trump was the focus of articles on his bad housing practices toward Blacks. In 1973, the U.S. Justice Department sued the young real estate businessman, his father, Fred, and Trump Management for housing bias. The Trumps were sued for allegedly not renting apartments to African Americans in one of the Trump developments. The practice was allegedly understood to be the rule within Trump Management where a "C" would be placed on the applications of minorities. Ultimately, Donald Trump counter-sued for millions. The case ended with a settlement and no admission of wrongdoing from the Trumps.

Trump has keenly understood the ramifications of his words and actions because he is one of the best self-marketers there is, knowing his name is his most valuable asset. If you think about it, a person's name is linked to their integrity and is the best asset (or biggest liability) for any person. But Trump understood its value at a different level. It was more than sacred; it was his larger-than-life brand that would carry him beyond New York real estate.

On Trump's road to the White House, birtherism, and its claim that Obama had been born in Kenya, sealed the deal on his latest and greatest venture. In September 2016, the businessman had to abandon the lie he had perpetuated and said in front of the media and all of America, "President Barack Obama was born in the United States." Trump's statement did not include an apology. Trump's admission that

Obama was not born in Kenya took years, but the damage had been done to President Obama. Trump was never taken to task and still won the presidency in 2016.

Fast-forward to January 20, 2017, Inauguration Day. That day is seared into my memory. The rebuke of the Obama administration was in full swing, with hate permeating from every nook and cranny of Washington, D.C. There was a weird mix of Trump supporters—some political, some fans, and others in a cultlike haze—who had come to DC to gloat at what they considered a momentous end to the reign of a Black man as president. Yes, it sounds very harsh, but it is true. Hillary Clinton had been defeated, and the countdown to President Obama's time as the country's leader was ticking away fast with only a few hours remaining. That day, orange became the new black.

You must remember Washington is a White, male-dominated fraternity for the most part, where men talk to men and when you don't look like that group, you are the outsider. When Obama was elected president, it was clear in Washington and other parts of this nation that he was unwanted. Broadcaster Rush Limbaugh and Senator Mitch McConnell are only two of the examples supporting this fact. And about 160 days or so into the Trump administration, it was evident that President Trump wanted to overturn anything President Obama achieved, from the Affordable Care Act (ACA) to thawing relations with Cuba to reforming the criminal justice system.

That Inauguration Day, I found a scattered, often sparse, crowd. It was the first time in over two decades that I could walk through an inauguration crowd so easily. The crowd was so scant that the bleachers around the White House were empty when I arrived early morning. They were still unoccupied following the traditional meetings of the vice president with the vice president-elect and then the president with the president-elect at the White House just before the oath of office on the steps of the U.S. Capitol.

The day was filled with hate, with challenges in the street between those vehemently against the incoming president and the small crowd of supporters on this historic inauguration with all this anticipation swirling. Everyone wondered what the next few years would look like. The clashes that day were loud and uncharacteristic of the historic nature of an Inauguration Day. Some of the protesters even wore masks and bandanas as a disguise. The masks were also handy for use against any type of gas that was dispersed by police and other agencies. What I clearly heard were flash-bangs to disperse crowds of protesters that day. It was concerning and scary. At one point, I could not distinguish between the twenty-one-gun salute and the flash-bangs to break up the crowd. It was a mosh pit of confusion, with a mix of protestors and those eager to see our democratic process play out.

Tensions were high, and the effort to peacefully transfer power went off-kilter a bit. Weeks prior to that day, which was highly anticipated by some and dreaded by others, President-elect Trump had tried to ease the tension from his campaign and had called President Obama for assistance in learning about the office he would occupy. When high-level staff were asked about how President Obama felt about the calls after months of hateful rhetoric, it is said that he chuckled. Mostly, he just wanted to move the country forward and help the incoming president. Obama had been extended that same assistance from his predecessor of the opposite party, George W. Bush. (Obama remains grateful to this day for Bush's efforts to help provide a seamless transition of power.)

January 20, 2017, was a cold day in Washington in attitude and temperature, with the thumb of President-elect Donald Trump in the eye of President Barack Obama. It started off with subtle defiance. Sources contend that minimal staff were on hand to assist in the traditional meeting of the old and new at the White House, and there were some unexpected surprises that went against protocol.

Per sources who were in the White House that day, when Vice President Joe Biden greeted incoming Vice President Pence, they were supposed to greet one another without posing for photographers. Well, Pence and his wife posed for pictures to the surprise of the Obamas. A source says that Mrs. Obama glanced at the staff as if to say, "This was not supposed to happen."

The next event that stirred emotions was a surprise gift for Mrs. Obama. On the surface, it was viewed as a nice gesture. It was later thought to be a public relations stunt by the Trumps to mend fences with Tiffany's, the tony New York City jewelry store in Trump Tower that had been hit hard economically by security barriers installed to protect the incoming First Family. Protocols were broken. Mrs. Melania Trump offered Mrs. Obama a gift in that pretty Tiffany's blue box with its stark white bow. A large, striking box like that would be allowed in most circumstances, but there were no staff available at that moment to take it. The First Lady awkwardly passed the box around her body and then President Obama took the gift inside and gave it to his social secretary who put the present in a box that was headed to their new Georgetown home just miles away. On the *Ellen* show in February 2018, Mrs. Obama said it was a "lovely [picture] frame."

I stood on the scaffolding press riser watching all this happen. I taped the entire meet-and-greet session, not knowing the backstory until a few months later. That was one of the moments seared into my memory like so many others. On certain occasions when I was near President Obama, I would study him closely, from the African design on his wedding ring to the freckles on his face to the veins in his hands to the crispness of his starched shirts. For President Trump, I have tried to do the same, from the coloring of his skin to the yellow of his hair that reminds me of corn silk.

Even with those unexpected pieces of information about the meet-and-greet, the day was historic. For sure, there were those who supported Trump and his views on immigration and other flashpoint issues. But there were also those who supported Trump simply because of his opposition to all things Obama. I saw it that day walking the streets, skinheads who felt they could come out of the shadows and practice their hate. Then you had the well-rounded, well-meaning people who justified their vote for Number 45 as a vote on the issues, not for the man. People wanted something new. They wanted something different. But people did not know exactly what that would look like.

On the other side of the political equation, people referred to Trump as Number 45 to avoid saying President Donald Trump. Many were uncomfortable having the person who had the loudest voice in the birther movement as the new president. The hypocrisy was so evident. Questions over Senator Ted Cruz being "legitimate" were not in the forefront because he was born in Canada from a Cuban father. Former governor Mitt Romney's dad was born in Mexico, and there were no questions there. But neither of them is Black. Race was and is the overwhelming factor regarding Obama!

In April 2017, President Trump admitted in an interview with Reuters that he thought being president "would be easier." That statement shook so many people as he said, "I loved my previous life. I had so many things going." Some former Obama administration staff and even everyday folks thought President Trump meant that if a Black man was able to do the job, then he could do it easily.

This president was not presidential in the traditional sense, and he was so different that he was not given sensitive intelligence that others had received. Barack Obama was given that information during sensitive intelligence meetings, sources and methods when appropriate. In contrast, there are questions about the depth of information President Trump receives as the national security advisor acknowledged that President Trump did not receive the most sensitive intelligence when he took part in a meeting with a Russian ambassador when he discussed the firing of FBI director James Comey. Trump was reportedly given sources and methods when it was deemed necessary.

Decades earlier, the thin, Black, Harvard-educated lawyer from Illinois took a different route to his presidency. He began with community activism and eventually was elected to the U.S. Senate and then the presidency. Along the way, his rise to power generated angst and resentment among other races, particularly Whites who did not approve of a Black man as their president. I have always referred to this phenomenon as a "Blacklash!"

This blacklash has come full circle with the rise of a novice to political office, Number 45, former businessman and now President Donald J. Trump. His name, his brand, has now extended to the White House. He appealed to people who felt left out and left behind over the last eight years. African Americans and those from other cultures heard what sounded like coded racism while others heard words that made them feel like they were part of the equation again. The reality is that even though it was 2017, Black people and many other groups had seen this before. What was so painful for some this time was that over the previous eight years, many learned of historic racial struggles but never actually felt the sting of racism. Others were lulled into a false sense of societal growth and progression, and naturally assumed that the atmosphere of acceptance would have enough momentum to sustain long after the first Black president left office. That is far from what has happened.

On that day, January 20, 2017, at 12:01 p.m., a new marker was set, the post-Obama era. What does it look like? The answer came almost immediately with issues of immigration, a travel ban, banning transgender persons from the U.S. military, riots in Charlottesville, concerns of where the administration stands on slavery and the Confederacy, the press being called "the enemy of the American People." The beginning weeks and months of the apprentice administration had many minority and ethnic groups living in fear that loved ones would be ripped from their families by the U.S. Immigration and Customs Enforcement agency and sent to home countries because of citizenship issues considered more of a crime than ever before.

The Trump administration believed a law was broken once a person has entered this country without proper documentation, no matter the reason. Also, residents of Muslim nations were now concerned that they may not be able to enter this country due to concern over Jihadist terrorist acts. Blacks were struggling with what law and order would look like now. Jewish Americans were concerned with the rise of anti-Semitism.

The nation was on edge.

· 2 ·

Healthcare Despair

*J*anuary 20, 2017, was the day Barack Obama left office and the new president assumed the post at 12:01 p.m. It was a day people worked to feel one another out, to see where we stood. Some basked in the light of the new day, the post-Obama era, the Trump era. What was going to happen first? Another kind of "change" had come to Washington. Some politicians, regardless of party, wanted to work with this neophyte crew on some very pressing issues affecting America.

During the inauguration luncheon on Capitol Hill, President Trump and veteran congressman Elijah Cummings, a Maryland Democrat, met up and agreed they should talk. For Congressman Cummings, this wasn't his first rodeo involving reaching across the aisle to make things happen, or at least trying to make things happen. The "thing" he wanted to address was the high cost of prescription drugs. At the luncheon, the new president seemed very concerned about this issue and wholeheartedly agreed they should talk. However, time passed and there was no follow-up. But the issue weighed on Elijah Cummings's heart. He thought he had his window of opportunity to begin discussions in earnest, but nothing was happening—radio silence on any connections.

I was curious about those early days and how the new occupant of the Oval Office was settling in. I wanted to know what his schedule was like. Was he overwhelmed? Was he stressed out? I could only imagine what it would be like for this man to assume such a lofty position following such an accomplished life. In my mind, he was probably doing his best to catch up on everything so that his staff and the American public would have confidence that he could handle the job. However, after I talked to a staffer who was there during those early days, things played out much differently than I could have ever imagined.

At that time, early in his administration, the president was using his "executive time" before, during, and after work. Start time for President Trump was generally 11:30 a.m. This was unheard of in the Bush and Obama administrations, or any other that I'm aware of. I checked in on their daily routines as well, and the latest they arrived at work was 8:30 a.m. It was not unusual for them to even begin the day at 7:30 a.m. or, obviously, sooner if there was a pressing issue. Those early meetings often allowed them to hold senior staff meetings and consultations with other world leaders who were in different time zones.

It was apparent from the beginning that this president was going to follow a completely different routine, one particularly focused on TV news. While President Trump resides in the shop above the store, he always seems to be watching television, especially at the time when MSNBC's *Morning Joe* news/talk show airs. One morning, the president saw Elijah Cummings on the air with Joe Scarborough and Mika Brzezinski. Congressman Cummings purposefully made mention of that Inauguration Day meeting. In true Trump fashion, the chief executive responded (for a change, not on Twitter). The president unexpectedly called Cummings, without any advance notice or warning.

I've known the congressman for a while, and he normally isn't shockable. But when one of his staffers reached him and said the president was on the phone, this time he *was* shocked. It is protocol to arrange the calls because both are busy men and may not be able to talk at the same time. With notice, both can prepare for the call and its agenda. Apparently, this new president was going to take a different approach, and the congressman adjusted. The two men finally discussed the issue of the high price of prescription drugs. They agreed to have a meeting because both men felt the issue was very important.

Well, what followed was a mess, and this may have been why protocol was not followed to arrange for a proper telephone meeting. The novice Trump staff just couldn't figure out how to pull the scheduling together. Since the meeting didn't happen right away, instead of investigating the cause, Trump went out at his first solo press conference and accused Congressman Cummings of not wanting the meeting and not liking him, once again turning a political issue and making it all about Trump. I knew that the former was far from the case. I especially knew this since I had been constantly reaching out to the congressman about if and when the meeting was to be scheduled. Cummings was more than eager to meet with the president, but the White House staff didn't seem to have their new office procedures together.

During President Trump's first press conference in office, as part of his answer to a question of mine, President Trump offered this response:

> Let's go set up a meeting. I would love to meet with the Black Caucus. I think it's great, the Congressional Black Caucus. I think it's great. I actually thought I had a meeting with Congressman Cummings and he was all excited. And then he said, "Well, I can't move, it might be bad for me politically. I can't have that meeting."
>
> I was all set to have the meeting. You know, we called him and called him. And he was all set. I spoke to him on the phone, very nice guy.

I replied: "I hear he wanted that meeting with you as well."
The president responded:

> He wanted it, but we called, called, called and can't make a meeting with him. Every day I walk and say I would like to meet with him because I do want to solve the problem. But he probably was told by Schumer or somebody like that, some other lightweight. He was probably told—he was probably told "Don't meet with Trump. It's bad politics."
>
> And that's part of the problem in this country. OK, one more [question].

What the president described couldn't have been true because I'd been hearing about the congressman's anticipation for the meeting every time I talked with him. From what I had discovered during my investigating, what the president said was just not accurate. This exchange was interesting for a couple of reasons. And Trump's exaggerations and total fabrications were confusing at first.

When he imagined the conversations that the congressman may have had with Senate Minority Leader Chuck Schumer, it was obviously not based in fact or truth. It was his way of lumping the two together and deciding, once again, that it was about him. I wasn't sure what to think of his response to my question because typically a sitting president would have talked about their initial conversation and that he was looking forward to continuing the dialogue, but not this president. This exchange was also my first true experience with becoming the story, and I'll get to that.

Finally, on March 8, 2017, after that first and only solo press conference of 2017, President Trump did meet, in the White House face to face, with Congressman Cummings to talk about lowering the cost of prescription drugs. Both sides said it was a good meeting. On the agenda for the meeting, Cummings offered this: "Allowing Americans to import their drugs from Canada and other places, mainly Canada. One of the other things you can do is to make sure that when it comes to patent laws, they are followed. A lot of these companies are holding out on patents and not allowing the new companies to come in that have a lower price."

However, it took almost a year for that issue to become a priority for this president. He mentioned it in his 2018 State of the Union speech in which he addressed Congress from the Well of the House.

In the meantime, the pharmaceutical industry was pushing back on Congressman Cummings's notion, and it continues to do so. They say they look to patent extensions to recoup their monies in a lot of cases, as a patent starts when they first discover a drug. A typical drug patent lasts fifteen to twenty years. Half of that time is eaten up in the development of a drug before it is on the market. Big Pharma also says about 80 percent of drugs sold are lower-priced generics.

So, back to the congressman's meeting with the president. Cummings says he also shared, "We have to look at our health agencies to make sure they are doing the right thing too. The other thing is to allow Medicare to negotiate the price of prescription drugs. Because Medicare is responsible for a huge percentage of the buying of prescription drugs. Those are the kinds of things that can help lower the price of prescription drugs."

Elijah Cummings demanded of President Trump, "You need to use the bully pulpit." He said of the high prices of drugs on the less fortunate, "This is murder on my people."

Again, it was my time to ask a question, *why is this murder?* According to the Baltimore congressman, "They may be able to get the care under Obamacare, but they can't get the cure. Essentially, you can go to the doctor, but you can't afford the pills the doctors prescribe."

I was curious about that because from what I had learned about the Affordable Care Act (ACA), there were provisions for access to medications. So even though I know the congressman and have a good working relationship with him, I still conducted my own research, because he and I both realize that particularly when it comes to the Black community, healthcare is life or death. In the Congressional Black Caucus book, *We Have a Lot to Lose*, it states:

> Under the Affordable Care Act, 60% of African Americans qualified for Medicaid, the Children's Health Insurance Program or premium subsidies to purchase insurance on the exchanges set up by the law.

We Have a Lot to Lose also says that

> Medicaid, which provides health insurance to low-income individuals, is a critical program on which millions of African Americans rely. Though African Americans make up only 13% of the American population, they account for 19% of those covered by Medicaid.

Reflecting on his session with the president, Elijah Cummings remembers the atmosphere of the room that day. He says that Tom Price, the then–Health and Human Services secretary, seemed "pissed that I was there because Republicans will complain about prescription drugs, but won't do anything about them."

The president called the congressman a day later and said, "We're working on it." (As of February 4, 2018, Cummings has not heard another word from the president on this issue.) The next day or a few days later, in typical Trump fashion, the president offered up a public comment about the meeting and said that Elijah Cummings had said he [Trump] "was the greatest president ever." Knowing Cummings as I do, that one did not pass the smell test. So, I called Cummings and asked, "What did you say?" I thought that possibly Cummings could have said something like, "You could be a great president *if . . .*"!

That "if" was a very substantial qualifier in the president's misinterpretation of what the congressman had said. Cummings told me that the president's words were not what he had said. Elijah Cummings was consistent, telling me the same thing when the news came out on that issue, then in February 2017, and again a year later when I was writing this book. Cummings said he told the president:

> You could be a great president if you do things for *all America* and not
> just the 35 or 36 percent that support you.

It was just amazing to me that Trump would take something like
that and turn it around, once again in favor of himself. I know you are
wondering if I believe Congressman Cummings over President Trump.
I do. I believe the congressman, but not based on any type of knee-jerk
reaction; it's based on my interactions with him over the years. I've
known him a long time, before he came to Congress. And I've never
heard anyone question what he says the way people question what President Trump says. I speak from personal experience: U.S. Congressman
Elijah Eugene Cummings is a stand-up man!

Trump's exercise in self-congratulation by changing what was said
did not surprise me, but it did help to confirm the pattern that was
emerging. In my years as a reporter, I had never seen anything quite like
it. While Congressman Cummings provided a logical, plausible expla-
nation for the exchange, President Trump's side once again didn't pass
the smell test.

Congressman Cummings also detailed to President Trump ways
that could make Trump a great president; for example, how Trump
could deal with the issue of "voting rights." And Cummings told the
president, "You viewed Black people as they can't do well. . . . And
stop talking about our communities being 'slaughter houses.'" In his
unabashed and truthful manner, Elijah Cummings told the president to
his face, "You have a large population that are scared."

That back and forth over what the congressman said overshadowed
the issue of lowering the cost of prescription drugs. Was that the president's goal all along? Did he know that by altering what had actually
happened he would be able to shift the focus away from the problem
by creating a controversy from it? I didn't get the impression he was
that strategic, but maybe he was. After all, he was able to convince an
entire swath of the population to vote for him, so he had learned a lot
on the campaign trail about what people responded to and what generated the most press for him.

The bright light in all of this is that the president has proclaimed
2018 as the year he will make lowering prescription drug prices a priority. Congressman Cummings is more than skeptical about the president's proclamation. He uses the example of the opioid crisis. This has

been a problem since well before we began hearing of its effects in Middle America during the 2016 presidential campaign. Elijah Cummings contends that a year into Trump's presidency, Trump could have done something by now. Cummings says he wants to wait and see what the president and the Republican Party will do, particularly because Kellyanne Conway is the new Opioid Czar who, at the initial efforts of combatting opioids, did not work with the Office of Drug Control Policy on the issue.

A politician's track record is typically how we make our determinations about a politician's promises and proclamations. What is his history? How have things played out for him in the past? Have there already been similar promises that were made without follow through? But Trump is no typical politician. Previously, not even politicians that lacked experience have conducted themselves in this way. They would consult with colleagues, hire experienced staff, and often tread cautiously until they were comfortable with the establishment.

We didn't have a political past to review, but we did have Trump's time on the campaign trail, something he obviously enjoyed and excelled at. There was a man named Kraig Moss who often showed up at the Trump rallies playing his guitar and singing pro-Trump songs. He was featured on many TV shows and news articles as "The Trump Troubadour." He was a prime example of that previously untapped voter from a rural area who felt disenfranchised, but Moss's mission was personal. He was campaigning for Trump in an effort to convince the presidential candidate to do something about the out-of-control opioid crisis.

Tragedy had struck Moss's own family when his son died of a heroin overdose. (Opioids are a class of drugs that include heroin, oxycodone, codeine, morphine, and fentanyl. According to the National Center on Drug Abuse, it is estimated that 23 percent of those who use heroin also develop opioid addiction.)

Since Trump touted himself as the everyman candidate, Moss followed him around and helped with the campaign. The highlight for him came when Trump talked to him from the stage at one of the rallies and assured him that something would be done about the crisis. He also asked the crowd to cheer for the fact that Moss was obviously "a great father," once again shifting the narrative. However, Moss made the mistake of taking Trump at his word, and he continued campaigning for

Trump. With all the press he received, he undoubtedly connected with the Trump base and helped convince them that Trump was their candidate.

A year later, the Trump Troubadour realized that nothing had been done, and he got the sinking feeling that nothing ever would be accomplished as far as managing the opioid crisis. He has since denounced Trump and even abandoned his moniker and is looking forward to championing a new candidate in 2020—Elizabeth Warren.

Armed with that history, I was curious as to whether anything would be done beyond the proclamation. Talk is cheap, as we all know. What if the president was really going to fight the high cost of prescription drugs? What would a fight with the White House against the pharmaceutical industry look like? For the most part, Big Pharma will stay quiet because much hinges on any word or comment from them. An example: When President Trump made his statement about lowering drug prices during his State of the Union speech, there was total silence from the industry. And when President Trump met with the heads of the pharmaceutical companies in 2017, he told them, "Healthcare is complicated." Again, radio silence from that industry on the president's seeming lack of knowledge of the pharmaceutical landscape. And when President Trump went after the African American head of Merck, Kenneth Frazier, the industry, and particularly Merck, was quiet. The president did not like that Frazier stepped down from the White House Manufacturing Council because of the president's comments on Charlottesville. We can also give the example of the efforts President Obama made with Obamacare. Back then, the industry was relatively quiet as well. This is another pattern that deserves attention.

Elijah Cummings says the only reason why the president wants to tackle drug prices now is because polls show 80 percent of Americans feel this is a top priority. Cummings says this is definitely not a Republican issue. But the overarching healthcare challenge is a major one for most, if not all, Americans. For our nation's Black community, Obamacare has been a help. Yes, there have been some problems, like high deductibles, the IRS assessing penalties, and the individual mandate. However, the Congressional Black Caucus believes the Affordable Care Act has been tremendous for expanding healthcare to African American individuals and families. According to *We Have a Lot to Lose*, the uninsured rate for nonelderly African Americans stands at 12 percent, four percentage points higher than the rate for White Americans. There are uninsured adults who fall into the coverage gap created by some states' refusal to expand Medicaid to those whose incomes are too high for Medicaid but not high enough to qualify for premium subsidies. Thirty percent of these uninsured adults are African Americans.

Let's be clear, Blacks were not the only target in this dismantling effort. Pediatricians have been concerned with how destroying healthcare insurance will affect the children they have been caring for. The effort by the Obama administration to pass the Affordable Care Act was so huge that Vice President Joe Biden was overheard on a hot microphone calling it "a big f—ing deal!" Obamacare is meant as a holistic approach to get people well. It is also meant to cut the number of folks using the emergency room as their doctor, which was creating extremely high hospital bills. In addition, it is about wellness, to maintain a reliable workforce that does not cost businesses with extensive use of sick days.

According to Anton Gunn, head of the Office of External Affairs at the U.S. Department of Health and Human Services in the Obama administration and a healthcare reform and leadership expert, when the Affordable Care Act was being formulated, "The uninsured rate of Black America was 27 to 28 percent." That was over a quarter of our Black population. The Obama administration understood that "if a rising tide lifts all boats you have to focus on the boats in the deepest water." People of color became the biggest beneficiaries of this new, targeted focus.

Anton Gunn says, "There isn't one major diagnostic area that is not prevalent or important in the African American community when it comes to disparities. So mental health, cancer treatment, stroke, HIV/AIDS, maternal [mother] and child health, cardiovascular disease, you just think about any chronic condition that is preventable or treatable. The disparities in the African American community is significant."

Gunn, who was with candidate Obama during Obama's first run for president, says the administration understood that "people of color, particularly Black Americans, have been chronically uninsured and have been since the inception of health insurance in America. We die sicker and quicker than other demographic groups because of the lack of health insurance coverage."

It's also a national security issue, Gunn explains. "Everybody that is in the United States of America has the ability to contribute. But when you have a significant portion of the population that is not physically healthy, and not mentally healthy, and their communities are not healthy, suffering from asthma, not having good water and good soil conditions. That makes people weak. And when that makes people weak, it makes Americans weak and it makes our nation weak." If we want to compete globally with the "best and brightest," Gunn says, we have to be on our game with our health.

During President George W. Bush's years in office, when his administration worked on issues of HIV/AIDS in Sub-Saharan Africa, the focus was on prevention and treatment and the issue of mother-to-child transmission. Then–Secretary of State Colin Powell called it a national security crisis. Powell made the point that if nations couldn't effectively sustain their military because of the HIV/AIDS health crisis, that was a problem that was a matter of national security. This problem would have ramifications on a global scale if any military engagement occurred.

As President Obama worked to lift all America, there was a definite positive impact on Black America. When we're hopeful, we see more possibilities. That administration won over Black America with the idea that our healthcare bills would be lower than our cell phone bills.

President Trump didn't see that. What he saw was President Obama's name attached to the Affordable Care Act. And he wasn't going to stand for that! Everyone knew that the ACA needed some tweaking, but it was helping people. Nevertheless, the ACA went on Trump's gilded chopping block. The ax was swift. It has already taken several swings to begin the dismantling the ACA, Obama's legacy, without any proposed replacement despite claims to the contrary.

There's something that warrants strong conversation: the benefits our poorest Americans received and didn't know what they were receiving. If you ask those in Appalachia if they liked the Affordable Care Act versus Obamacare, there is a frightening fact that has been discovered from studies and reports. These poverty-stricken White Americans, hands down, *scream how much they love the Affordable Care Act and hate Obamacare.* To further reinforce this point, here's something from a *New York Times* article from February 7, 2017, titled "One Third Don't Know Obamacare and Affordable Care Act Are the Same," by Kyle Dropp and Brendan Nyhan:

In the survey, 35 percent of respondents said either they thought Obamacare and the Affordable Care Act were different policies (17 percent) or didn't know if they were the same or different (18 percent). This confusion was more pronounced among people 18 to 29 and those who earn less than $50,000—two groups that could be significantly affected by repeal.

Among Republicans, a higher percentage (72 percent) said they knew Obamacare and the A.C.A. were the same, which may reflect the party's longstanding hostility to the law.

Of course, we are aware that the two laws are one and the same thing. Republicans changed the name of the Affordable Care Act to smear both that law and President Barack Obama. To the Republicans' dismay, the president embraced the word *Obamacare* by saying, "Yes, Obama Cares!" It was yet another attack on the monumental accomplishment of getting the law passed in the first place. There had been previous efforts, but it wasn't until Obama that it became a reality.

It's alarming that in our country there is such a struggle to ensure that citizens can obtain healthcare. Since there is some confusion about the name of the law, I find it's best to lay out definitions and clarifications to ensure that everyone is on the same page. (I don't have time for fake news.) According to the World Health Organization (WHO), "Universal Health Coverage exists when all people receive the quality health services they need without suffering financial hardship." That seems like a basic need that is required to survive, so why is it so difficult to obtain?

As the leader of the free world, it's a travesty that we have to struggle and debate and legislate the issue of ensuring that our citizens are healthy. WHO ranked the world's health systems, with France coming out in the top spot, followed by Italy and the United States at 37, between Costa Rica and Slovenia. So, what's the answer? How do we improve our healthcare, insure those who need it the most, and provide excellent care?

The fact is that not everyone agrees that universal healthcare should be the goal. That's where the conversation needs to begin. First, there needs to be enough research to determine the best approach. Many people think that the system we now have works because it is profit based and that motivates caregivers to perform better than if the same care is given to everyone.

One thing everyone can agree on is that healthcare is expensive no matter how you look at it. France is rated the highest, but according to various reports, that high ranking comes at a financial cost. Some reports claim they have the second highest healthcare expenditure in the world. The other four countries with the expensive healthcare price tags are Germany, the Netherlands, and Sweden. However, the correlation with France's expenses and their high ranking does not always work. The Netherlands ranks at number 17 among world health systems, with Sweden at 23 and Germany at 25. So, expense doesn't necessarily mean the best quality.

The Organization for Economic Cooperation and Development (OECD) released a report in 2015 that detailed the annual per capita healthcare costs of various countries. In it, it was reported that the United States spends around $8,713 per person annually for healthcare, which was higher than any other country, regardless of ranking.

No matter your political affiliation, the ACA should be acknowledged as a step in the right direction. It was something of a compromise between our current system and a universal option. The goal was to provide everyone with access to the current system based on what they could afford. Admittedly, the solution was not perfect, far from it, but it was an attempt, and even that took huge compromise. At least it was something to work with, a place to begin bringing some equalizing to our system that favors those in the higher income brackets.

And here's an old argument, but so true. If there was such disdain for the ACA, why didn't the GOP have something ready to replace it when they gained the White House, the House, and the Senate and were sworn in in 2017? When we're talking about people's lives, that's not the time for political gamesmanship. There was rightful angst and concern during the rollout of the ACA website when it broke down on day one and couldn't handle the web traffic on the site. The issue was including multiple government contracts that didn't allow for an integration of ideas for the system. The administration understood how serious this matter was. Senior White House officials like Chief of Staff Denis McDonough and the head of Health and Human Services supervised the efforts to work out the kinks. The president didn't visit the project where the fixing was being done, but he called in and videoed into the inner sanctum to ensure his legacy piece would work after all the hiccups.

Still, the mere fact that the website could not handle the traffic shows just how important it was to so many people. They were clamoring for the information, and the demand was so great that the newly christened site couldn't meet the demand. It was explained to me that it was like a Black Friday sales event with a rush of people trying to cram into the front door. The system could not handle the mad rush, so it broke. I'm not sure there is a better barometer than that in this digital age.

Anton Gunn notes that health issues in the Black community are more severe, and that's true in every category. Because of these issues there was a hard-fought effort in the Obama administration to target Black and Brown America with Obamacare. It was a necessary move. From heart disease, to diabetes, to sickle cell, to cancer and beyond, Black and Brown America are hit hard compared with White America.

President Trump has constantly worked to dismantle the Affordable Care Act, and at some point, he will try to end it. Anton Gunn explains that the ACA isn't simple legislation but a very complex piece of public policy. Trump has been able to dismantle things in some areas. However, there are other areas that his administration hasn't touched because they don't understand what's in the law. Gunn says hospitals are already implementing ways to improve on care that the ACA has brought about.

He says, "They are not gonna go backward. . . . They can repeal the Affordable Care Act all they want. Hospitals are still going to document the quality metrics and deliver quality care for people."

The alarming part of this is that the previously untapped votes, the "forgotten man," as we have referred to them, was a large benefactor of ACA (and even Obamacare, but we won't mention that). So, those who so strongly supported getting Trump into office are now paying the price by no longer being able to afford healthcare due to changes that have occurred.

That means those uninsured people will end up being a burden on the system and will eventually cost taxpayers, one way or another. At some point, they will require healthcare and the hospital will provide it. If the bill goes unpaid, it will move to collections and affect the patient's credit and the hospital's bottom line. Eventually that will mean the patient may even need to declare bankruptcy. A Harvard University study found that medical expenses were the leading cause for personal bankruptcy filings at 62 percent. And those bankruptcies eventually impact the economy.

Reporting from my unique perch, as I write these pages, I have seen that the issue of race touches everything. Racism has had an impact on healthcare for Black America since the beginning. To demonstrate this, I would like to share with you two stories my late mother told me as a kid that have remained with me. One is the story of the Tuskegee Syphilis Study in which Black men who were infected with this disease were used like laboratory rats for experimentation. This atrocity has resulted in mistrust of the healthcare system by Blacks, so we're not eager to take part in clinical trials to this day. This is true, although there are new standards and accountabilities that should prevent anything like this happening again. Even so, this deadly experiment left scars on generations.

The other story is about the impact of racism and segregation before the Civil Rights Act. Charles Drew, a Black man, invented the modern system for blood donation, transportation, and storage! He invented the bloodmobile. Most of us have benefited from blood transfusion, and many of us have had our lives saved thanks to Charles Drew. At the time Drew made his momentous advance in medical treatment, this nation was almost completely segregated by race. When the Civil Rights Act finally came in 1964, it allowed African Americans to stay in public accommodations, use public bathrooms, eat in restaurants, and use the same hospitals.

Dr. Drew's daughter, Charlene Drew Jarvis, told me this story at a White House event during the Obama years. In 1950, Dr. Drew was driving down South in North Carolina. However, because of racism he could not lay his head on a pillow in any hotel, and he fell asleep at the wheel. The accident occurred near the city of Burlington. He was taken to a hospital, to the basement, to the Black ward. A White doctor recognized who Drew was and took him upstairs to where White patients were treated. Unfortunately, Charles Drew never regained consciousness, and he died of his severe injuries. Here we have a man who helped all people, of all races and backgrounds, with his medical and scientific brilliance. Just imagine if he had lived what more he could have done to revolutionize medicine. Racism has no place in any society. We all lose out!

Ultimately, the healthcare issue should be a universal one, not relegated to one political party or another. It's a fact that many other countries have been able to figure out a way to provide their citizens with healthcare so that no one is left out. Most of the systems are different, ranging from complete universal care, to hybrids that include public and private providers. The point is not that one size fits all, but that the solutions are out there, and other countries are finding them.

In 2016, the Obama White House put out a fact sheet about the progress that the ACA had made:

> On March 23, 2010, President Obama signed the Affordable Care Act (ACA) into law, putting in place comprehensive reforms that improve access to affordable health coverage for everyone and protect consumers from abusive insurance company practices. Today, the ACA is working: thanks to the ACA, 17.6 million previously uninsured people had gained coverage prior to this year's open enrollment period, and the law has driven the uninsured rate below 10 percent—for the first time since we started keeping records. The ability to buy portable and affordable plans on a competitive marketplace is giving Americans the freedom to move, start businesses and dream big American dreams, which is especially important as more consumers become entrepreneurs. And thanks in part to the law's focus on reducing costs and inefficiencies, health care prices have risen at the slowest rate in 50 years since the law passed, which will benefit all of us for years to come.

The benefits of the ACA were clearly listed, including:

- Some 17.6 million consumers have gained health insurance. From 2010 through the first nine months of 2015, the uninsured rate has fallen by more than 40 percent and, for the first time ever, more than nine in ten Americans now have health insurance. In Wisconsin, Gallup recently estimated that the adult uninsured rate in 2015 was 5.9 percent, down from 11.7 percent in 2013.
- As many as 129 million Americans who have some type of pre-existing health condition, including up to 19 million children, are now protected from coverage denials and reduced benefits—practices that were routine before the law's enactment.
- Some 105 million Americans, including 39.5 million women and nearly 28 million children, have benefited from annual limits on

out-of-pocket spending on essential health benefits—and the elimination of lifetime and annual limits on insurance coverage. These are protections that did not exist before the ACA.

- Americans now have access to critical preventive services at no cost, like flu shots, yearly check-ups, and birth control. These are benefits that did not exist before the ACA.

- Over 14 million more Americans have received coverage through Medicaid since the ACA's first open enrollment period in 2013. States have an option to expand Medicaid to all non-eligible adults with incomes under 133 percent of the federal poverty level, and to date, thirty-one states and the District of Columbia have chosen to expand the program. In these states that have already expanded Medicaid, 4.4 million uninsured people will gain coverage. If the remaining states expand Medicaid, over 4 million more uninsured people would gain coverage.

- The ACA has provided new transparency in how health insurance plans disclose reasons for premium increases and requires simple, standardized summaries so over 170 million Americans can better understand their coverage information and compare plans. These consumer protections did not exist six years ago.

- Some 2.3 million young Americans gained coverage between 2010 and October 2013 because they could now stay covered on their parents' healthcare plans until they turn twenty-six, a benefit that did not exist before the law.

- The ACA created tax credits that, as of September 2015, have helped 7.8 million Americans who otherwise often could not afford to purchase health coverage through the health insurance marketplaces.

- Health insurers are now required to provide consumers with rebates if the amount they spend on health benefits and quality of care, as opposed to advertising and marketing, is too low. Last year, 5.5 million consumers received nearly $470 million in rebates. Since this requirement was put in place in 2011 through 2014, more than $2.4 billion in total refunds will have been paid to consumers.

- Out-of-pocket costs have been eliminated for preventive services like immunizations, certain cancer screenings, contraception, reproductive counseling, obesity screening, and behavioral assess-

ments for children. This coverage is guaranteed for more than 137 million Americans, including 55 million women.
- Out-of-pocket costs have been eliminated for 39 million Medicare beneficiaries for preventive services like cancer screenings, bone-mass measurements, annual physicals, and smoking cessation.
- The ACA expands mental health and substance use disorder benefits and parity protections to over 60 million Americans.
- The ACA phases out the "donut hole" coverage gap for nearly 10.7 million Medicare prescription drug beneficiaries, who have saved an average of $1,945 per beneficiary.
- Accountable Care Organizations (ACOs) now exist, consisting of doctors and other healthcare providers who come together to provide coordinated, high-quality care at lower costs to their Medicare patients. Over 477 ACOs are serving nearly 8.9 million Medicare beneficiaries nationwide.
- Overpayments through the Medicare Advantage system have been phased out, while Medicare Advantage plans are required to spend at least 85 percent of Medicare revenue on patient care. Medicare Advantage enrollment has grown by 50 percent to over 17.1 million while premiums have dropped by 10 percent since 2009.
- Hospitals in Medicare now receive incentives to reduce hospital-acquired infections and avoidable re-admissions. A collaborative health-safety learning network, the Partnership for Patients, includes more than 3,200 hospitals to promote best quality practices.

I do realize that the report is intended to highlight the successes and not focus on the problems that were also experienced, but I found the statistics important and appreciated the fact that they were backed up by studies (which I didn't include here). That's the way we can make an intelligent, informed decision about the future of healthcare in this country. It's not based on who initiated the legislation or how one lawmaker feels about another, it's about the people of the United States.

If the ACA wasn't perfect, at least it was a beginning. It was a starting point. Since it was able to make the difficult journey into law, it should not be carelessly disregarded and dismantled. It should be examined, studied, and improved upon. Now that we have over seven years of real-world use, those studies and statistics can help guide the way to a solution that works for everyone, regardless of income level or race.

Our health and the health of our country depend on it.

· 3 ·

Becoming the Story

$\mathcal{T}$he year 2017 was full of news, with the Muslim ban, the efforts to repeal Obamacare, the end of net neutrality, the ban on transgender people serving in the military, governance through "official" tweets of the president, and the war of words regarding North Korea's nuclear capability, numerous Trump administration staff firings, and Gold Star deaths in Niger. Also in the news were the first "wins" for the president with the appointment of Supreme Court Justice Neil Gorsuch and the passage of tax reform legislation. There was so much news to report, and yet I often wound up becoming the story.

You've seen it! The combative responses of the president and his press secretaries to my questions; the White House's attempts to discredit me; the condescending and demeaning comments by administration staff; the falsehoods and insults hurled at me by total strangers—replayed thousands of times and now residing in cyberspace: the memes, GIFs, news clips, and viral videos. What boggles my mind more than the social media frenzy is that people constantly ask me: "How were you able to sit there and take it?" What choice did I have? It's part of my job. Over the years "taking it" has morphed into that.

On September 22, 2017, at the Black Women's Agenda Luncheon at the Marriott Marquis Hotel, during Congressional Black Caucus Legislative Week, I received the Education Award. I was being honored along with Senator Kamala Harris. At the head table, Senator Harris was seated on my right. She turned to me, leaned over the person between us, and said with bewilderment and a sisterly smile of support, "You keep going back!"

Without thinking, I said, "So do you!" I also gave her this truth: "I keep going back because I did nothing wrong!"

My conversation with Senator Harris was my first real-life indication to what extent what had been happening to me was reaching everyone. People were seeing how this new administration was treating people like me—with aggression and condescension. At first, I thought maybe the seemingly nonstop media coverage of these incidents was just a social media type of thing that would blow over, but it did not. It just kept going, and incident upon incident continued with this White House and its press secretaries. I have even had to fight for my professional life against the potentially career-ending lies and harsh, aggressive words from a person from the Trump campaign who then "worked" in the White House and then was forced to "resign." In this chapter and subsequent ones, I'll go into detail about these events and others.

I continue to go back to the White House and do my job—the job I've been doing for more than two decades. As I said, I've done nothing wrong. And I'm covered by the First Amendment of the U.S. Constitution. I'm sure that when the Founding Fathers drafted this pillar for our nation, they had no idea there would be a White House press corps, let alone a Black woman as a member. They would never know that this Black woman would lean on the Constitution for support while being embroiled in a back and forth with the White House over serious journalistic questions, not to mention being accused of having her own agenda to discredit the administration.

I work in the White House with reverence and respect, but the daily struggle to sustain my respect is real. And there is collateral damage. The daily struggle affects not only me but also my loved ones, who watch the briefings and are concerned for me. But most of all, I hate how my kids are affected by this. It's been so bad that when the viral videos and news clips happen, their school has to rally around to protect them from any venom that may follow. One of the most positive things is that they see their mom is okay. Then my kids walk with their heads held high and move through life as if it's a singular moment that doesn't last long.

I'm a person who does not focus on her own press releases and public relations. I just do my job and try not to think too much about my accomplishments and not-so-stellar moments. However, the pressure can be overwhelming. We'll get into all that, but typically people either get tired of the White House beat after the hard swings, are fired, or are reassigned to cover something else. None of the above were options for me. I was there for three prior administrations. So why was I such a problem? Seriously, why?

There were moments when I wanted to give up, and I seriously contemplated throwing in the towel, so I understood why people asked how I could take it. They probably imagined what they would have done in my situation. Most probably they wouldn't have stayed. To be clear, I didn't sign up to be the object of harassment. But I knew that if I left, I would have been viewed as a quitter. I had worked too hard for this job. Also, I stand on too many proud shoulders of people from all races and walks of life. I won't let some foolishness end my asking questions on topics other reporters don't think to ask. If it's not me interjecting with those pointed questions, then who else in that prestigious room of very aggressive individuals will step up?

I have worked through several White House transitions of power, and I know what it is like. I understand how the outgoing occupant is trying to have a dignified exit that the leader of the United States deserves while the incoming president is eager to set his own tone, make a name for himself, and prove that the voters made the right choice. It's typically a delicate dance, with both sides showing respect and reverence to the other, or at least civility.

I had hope for my relationship with the new administration; more specifically, the press secretary with whom I would have to work in the White House briefing room. Regardless of political party, I have always tried hard to develop a connection with the new officials, hoping to establish a good working relationship. My job depends on their cooperation, and they look to me to report accurately without interjecting my personal feelings, and that's what I do. Often I actually enjoy working with folks, from both sides of the aisle, with whom I don't necessarily agree politically. I want to understand all sides of an issue so that I can accurately report on them.

That's why I have to ask those questions. Any White House administration will present things in the best light for them, so it's up to me to dig deeper, to question them and see how they respond to someone who might have a different take on the subject. For some reason, now that I'm much more visible, people don't realize that I've been doing this a long time and that I do the same regardless of the administration. I have to dig for answers because no White House wants to present everything right up front. It just doesn't work that way. The journalists in the room must come prepared for whatever is thrown at them. They have to decide how they should respond, and then they have to do it.

It's not as easy as it may seem. I never expected that I would end up being someone that people see as their only true representation in that room. There are other minorities there, but I have been singled out and labeled as the only Black female reporter in the White House briefing room. What really matters to me, what I've come to realize, and what people have told me, is that they look to me to represent them. Those who feel disenfranchised or left out want me to question what is being said and done within the current administration. I was doing the same job with the previous president, but I think because he was Black, people didn't see the racial aspect as much when I would ask a question.

It's very clear that with the Trump administration, the race lines have been drawn. I have a responsibility to question on matters that a certain swath of people want answers for. They are counting on me to come at an issue from a different angle, to ask how it will affect people that may not have been considered previously. I cannot adequately express to you how seriously I take that responsibility. I want to get answers, not engage in verbal volleys about things that don't really matter.

So, if I don't have a decent relationship with the press officers, they are not likely to call on me, and then I can't do my job. I'm sure it looks easy on television, but asking those questions can be stressful and difficult. I never want to be rude or embarrass them. I just want the facts. I have to come up with a question that I can ask quickly, one that is presented in a way that they will answer. Believe me, it is work.

When members of the current administration started firing back at me, I was startled at first because I hadn't seen that level of aggression in previous administrations. I was surprised that I was being addressed in that way. I wasn't shocked, because not much can shock me these days, but I was surprised. What did I do in response? I had to fight back. The challenge was, how was I going to fight back against a group of people with such a large megaphone? I think every answer for me in this scenario drew on a common-sense, streetwise approach. As a kid growing up in Baltimore, I was always told by my Aunt Pearl, who continues to tell my kids to this day, "When you're being bullied, hit the bully one good time and they'll leave you alone."

During the 2016 presidential campaign, I saw the truth in that statement. The Trump campaign played a street game, and not the traditional game of politics. One of the first examples of that was how the Trump campaign went after Hillary Clinton. They publicly called this esteemed and accomplished woman names like "Crooked Hillary," and those names stuck. The Trump camp was effective in the smear. Secretary Clinton wanted to stay above the fray and not get down in the gutter. However, the truth is that a different variety of politics was in play. She needed to strike back.

Donald Trump, not being a true Republican or a traditional politician, had her constantly off her game with his folly. He always had her on the defensive. She didn't know what his strategy was and didn't seem prepared for it. For that matter, the nation was stunned as well. Watching how Hillary Clinton handled Donald Trump on the campaign trail was riveting and taught me a valuable lesson. I was taking note as a reporter and ultimately as a person who had to devise my own method of play.

To be fair, Hillary Clinton was no stranger to different and new challenges during this campaign season. Bernie Sanders threw her camp off-kilter at the beginning because he was not a traditional Democrat. However, Sanders was nothing like Trump. Sanders was of the far left, but he did not play gutter games. But when it came to Trump, Clinton didn't fight back against the bully. Not even when he towered and hovered over her at the debate where he brought the sexual abuse accusers of her husband, Bill Clinton, to sit in the audience and watch the debate up close. It was a dirty political trick, and the intimidation factor was high that night. Trump fought her like it was hand-to-hand combat, with no mercy.

I learned a valuable lesson from Secretary Clinton during her campaign against candidate Trump. I learned that sometimes it's best to take the high road and let others speak for you. Yes, Mrs. Obama is right, "When they go low, we go high." But other times the only person who can really defend you against the lies and attacks against your character is you! There are times you must meet bullies at their level and be louder than they are if you want to survive savage attacks on your integrity, character, and career in this hostile political climate.

My issues with the administration started long before Trump found his way to the White House. I knew someone from the new staff previously. There was one person with whom I had established a casual friendship with—Omarosa Manigault-Newman. It did not end well.

After the events began to unfold, and I learned more about her, I realized that I was in a so-called friendship with a duplicitous person. I cringe even when I think about it. What was most upsetting to me was the fact that I had overlooked the signs of who she really was. Whenever I asked about dubious events or negative things I'd heard that she had done or was doing, she would always come up with some sort of plausible, twisted-sounding excuse. As for me, although her explanations were questionable, I would say, "okay." After all, we were supposedly friends, so I was trying to be a good, supportive friend. However, when she joined the Trump campaign, it caused me to really take stock of what was going on.

After she had been offered a position in the campaign, the reporter in me came out, and I asked her, "How as a Black woman can you support a candidate that uses code words against the minority community?" She gave the excuse of being "loyal" to him and that she knew "he is crazy." She also said she would be the only one "in there to help the Black community." There were others in our friendship circle who seemed to accept her explanations as well. Deep down in my spirit I knew something wasn't right. We shared, but it was never that deep and personal. I guess I didn't want to consciously admit to myself that she had another side.

You may not realize that when I met her, I thought she was controlled and professional, not the bombastic *Apprentice* TV show personality. And even after she began appearing on the show, she would say, "Oh, you know that's just the character I play."

I first met Omarosa Manigault in the 1990s, during the last years of the Clinton administration when she worked in the office of Vice President Al Gore. Whenever we interacted, she would ask me to do interviews with Vice President Gore. We were both younger in spirit and looks. She was in her early twenties and wore an Afro then and seemed to be kind. I remember that when she would call, I couldn't understand her name when she introduced herself. I had never heard that name before, and I wouldn't say it because I was so unsure of its pronunciation.

We only had cursory conversations when she called to set up the interviews. We mouthed pleasantries when we crossed each other's paths on the White House campus grounds. Little did I know at the time that she had sharp elbows, even back then. I am told she caused constant confusion in the vice president's office and that she also caused problems within the West Wing, calling at least two people racist. Managers had to step in and calm the situation. Sources who worked as staff in the Clinton White House have confirmed that she "failed out." This dressed-up term essentially means she was fired from the White House. Sources refer to her time there as a "nanosecond." Subsequently, she was moved over to the Commerce Department and the Democratic National Committee. My sources are not firm on which organization she went to first after being fired by the White House, but they revealed these were the two most immediate jobs she held after the Clinton White House exit. And then she was out of the government workforce altogether.

So, after the White House and her many jobs, Omarosa and I didn't cross each other's paths until after her appearances on *The Apprentice*. We connected again and exchanged numbers, and sort of kept in touch, but not in a major way. But during the Obama years, our friendship evolved into hanging out in different cities when we were at the same event or just in each other's neighborhood. I even went to a Baltimore church once to hear her preach.

Let's fast forward to the summer of 2016. Again, I thought I had a friend, and I'm deliberately using the word *thought*. We often talked and even met each other's family and friends. Well, everything was fine until I got in the way of what her boss wanted, which was to attack the press. I was a prime target for her. In her eyes, she could solidify her standing with the group of folks she worked with, the ones who were leery of her. She had been a Bill Clinton–, Barack Obama–, and Hillary Clinton–supporting Democrat before she became a Trump supporter and turned into a Republican conservative. Like Trump, she was another DTR. If she served me up on the platter to her "friend," as she called "DT," it would show that she was really "one of them" and that she was in the DT camp for real. If this scenario had played the way she had wanted, she would easily have secured trust in that camp and better solidified her tenuous position. However, the only person in her corner was Donald Trump; the rest were suspicious of her.

I soon learned that what we had was not friendship at all. When she tried to play her games with me, I did not tolerate it. She had mistaken my kindness for weakness, and that was not the right move for her to make. She tried to set me up along the way, but I didn't take the bait. She tried to "status climb" in the Trump campaign by lying about a well-known and well-positioned, long-standing White House correspondent. I reported to a group of people who were not the base constituency of Donald J. Trump.

When I think back to all of that, it reminds me of the words of a gospel song: "We come this far by faith, Leaning on the Lord." I had come too far to let this charlatan damage my life, the life of my kids, and the credibility of my character and my career.

I recall times during the campaign when she was a Trump surrogate and I was on MSNBC quite often, on Chris Matthews's *Hardball*. When she offered information for me to use on TV and I didn't use it, she would ask me why. I would say that I wanted to keep our friendship separate from our professional lives. Frankly, by then I didn't trust her. I realized that only a kernel of what she said was true and the rest was wrong or even a lie. She tried several times to feed me information to use when I had a national platform on TV so that I could do her bidding, but I never fell for that. Also during that time, she said the campaign was keeping dossiers on three highly vocal Blacks: Jamal Bryant, Roland Martin, and me.

Omarosa's life changed during the summer of 2016 when she found a man to marry. We were close enough at that time for her to consider me as an attendant at her wedding. I received the text from her: "I said yes to him! Now will you say yes to me? Be my bridesmaid?" I never gave her a firm answer as it just did not sit well with me. Here I was, an unbiased journalist, and what message would it send from me? I would be participating in the wedding of a person who worked for a man I openly questioned regarding his divisive campaign rhetoric. I wasn't sure how to handle the unexpected invitation since I had always been so careful about not mixing my personal and professional life. It was always crucial that I remain impartial and avoid putting myself in any situation that could seem as if I supported one political side or another.

It became increasingly difficult to avoid her constantly approaching me to get a commitment to be her bridesmaid. I tried to avoid her and that bridesmaid question. I thought she was just talking from excitement. I never gave her an answer, but I was supportive of her new life. Yet at the same time, I was very vocal in how I didn't like the racial dog whistles coming from her candidate to pump up his base.

Have you ever had the type of friend that you just couldn't read? One minute you think you have a good relationship, and then she will say or do something that totally changes your opinion? That's what it was like. I always felt like there was an agenda, some underlying reason for everything she said or did, as if it was yet another move in her reality-show strategy to life. Then with the bridesmaid invitation, I couldn't tell if she was sincere, if she was trying to set me up, or if she just wanted to use my attendance to show that she had a friend in the press. I had no idea what she was telling Trump or the others she worked with, so I thought my best approach was to just leave it alone and see how our relationship would progress. Then came Wikileaks.

Apparently via the Russians, Wikileaks had gotten hold of the emails of John Podesta, Hillary Clinton's campaign manager. It was understandable that mixed in with the more controversial emails would be communications with and about journalists. And as I suspected, there were emails from me in there. I had asked the campaign for a meeting between Hillary Clinton and Black journalists, trying to figure out why the Black base was not as energized as other Democrats thought they should be. At the same time, I was asking the Trump campaign (through Omarosa and calls to Trump Tower and Trump's secretary) for the same, a meeting and interview with candidate Trump. I even publicly went on Twitter asking the candidate himself for interviews. No response. In any event, my emails to the Trump campaign were not reflected in the trove of Podesta emails and in the news accounts.

News stories came out about my name being mentioned in those emails. According to mutual friends, Omarosa was upset that I was in any of those emails. And this is where Omarosa thought she had a clear chance to pounce. She devised a scenario that went like this: Omarosa began saying that I was taking money from the Hillary Clinton campaign! She then reported this lie to a mutual friend who later told me that he had told her that she was reading the news stories wrong and that she was misinterpreting the emails.

Omarosa is a smart person, and she understood what the news articles were saying, but she wanted to twist the stories to make me appear guilty of being an unethical journalist. She told this to many people. I even received an email from Russia TV asking for an interview about my involvement in the Podesta emails. Interestingly, plenty of news media were discussing the emails, but the Russians were the only news outlet asking me about them. I was getting angry then. Just months prior to this email controversy, Omarosa had mentioned on several occasions that I should try to go on foreign television and that I would get paid a good deal of money. What she did not know was that several foreign news agencies have called me from time to time over my career to make appearances. I have done several foreign news networks like the BBC (and was paid by one foreign outlet). Over the years. I never dealt with Russia TV. I found her conversation so coincidental.

I was on the set of *Meet the Press* on October 11, 2016. Between segments, I received a Twitter direct message on my phone from a lawyer friend of Omarosa, one of her bridesmaids. Then the woman called me and said the story was everywhere, and she would represent me if I needed it. I said, "The only people you heard that from was Omarosa and her circle, and I don't need any representation." I said, "Thanks," and hung up. Yet another of Omarosa's ploys.

I was shocked by the call, but I didn't put it all together until days later. Omarosa's friend had represented a very famous person in a high-profile case. If I had said yes to her representation, just to have her as a lawyer, Omarosa, of course, would be the first to know. This would signify guilt and imply some sort of wrongdoing on my part. That would give Omarosa and her boss, candidate Trump, a lot to say about it publicly and further perpetuate the lies and his "fake news" mantra. It became clear that this was a devious and underhanded plan to, at the least, humiliate me and, at most, sabotage my career. I began to radically distance myself from Omarosa and her friends.

At that point, I certainly did not want to be in her wedding and was trying to figure out how I could sever the friendship altogether. Naturally, she was oblivious, or played the part, because she still wanted me as a bridesmaid! Around Thanksgiving 2016, she and her fiancé Face Timed me, asking me to be in the wedding and pressing for an answer. I told them that I had something else to discuss. With the three of us on the chat session, I did ask her fiancée if he knew what had happened regarding her claims that I allegedly had taken money from Hillary Clinton's campaign. Omarosa cut in and said, "I don't get John involved with my work." When I proceeded to say something about the incident, she said, "You know I will protect you." How Machiavellian!

The lack of communication and time that had passed placed even more stress on the relationship. When Trump became president-elect, folks were jockeying for position in that camp, and I began hearing even more than usual about her. I was in New York one day and wanted to meet with her to warn her she was still a target of the insiders in the Trump camp. But she became arrogant and defensive. She also claimed to be covered by "the blood of Jesus."

Later, I remember talking with that same lawyer friend, who said Omarosa kept talking about the warnings I had delivered. At that moment, the friend unknowingly affirmed it was not casual conversation for them. They were discussing me and everything I was doing. As far as I was concerned, my friendship with Omarosa was completely over. I had been telling folks since October 2016 about what was being said and how shocked I was by each new statement. Me, taking money from any political candidate? Girl, bye!

So, we barely talked during the time of the presidential transition. I actually told her I was happy for her. She was getting everything she wanted, but at the same time I wanted out of the trap. I even said to her, "When I see you on campus, I'll act like I don't know you." That didn't sit well with her. She took offense. I really was not feeling anything about her at the time.

Donald Trump became president, and Omarosa was back in the White House, this time under a Republican administration. I must give her credit for that. She was managed out of the Clinton White House and somehow, she had wormed her way back in. If nothing else, that was an impressive show of sheer determination, but was it a smart move? Knowing her employment history, I was interested to see how it would play out.

The first press briefing day, she was looking for me. She text-messaged me, asking where I was so that she could meet up with me. I was not going to miss the briefing, but I was not sitting around the White House waiting either. From the internal White House video stream of the briefing room, she could see that I was not sitting in my seat. I told her I would be there soon. Once I got situated, she came out of the press room door and gave me the peace sign before the briefing started. I found it so funny because the rest of the room thought it was the two-minute warning for the briefing to begin. I said no. It was the peace sign. That's Omarosa, and yet another of her lost-in-translation moments. But even as she was trying to be cool with me, she was working behind the scenes, telling newly appointed press secretary Sean Spicer and others not to acknowledge me or call on me.

Meanwhile, the day of the first Trump White House press briefing, I was pleasantly surprised when I was the fifth person Spicer called on, but that momentum was cut short. February 2017 came around, Black History Month! For me it was the month when it all came to a head! The White House wanted that month to demonstrate the course correction with the Black community. The effort was pulled together by President Trump's dutiful friend and loyal employee, Omarosa. That entire month was originally set aside to celebrate a community that was still struggling for first-class citizenship in a host of categories. However, the month was fraught with problems. beginning with the controversy over identifying and naming the month.

Around February 2, I received a frantic email from someone in the civil rights community pointing my attention to a leaked proclamation and the title of a story on TMZ. Someone leaked the Black History Month proclamation to TMZ and said Trump had 86'ed Black History Month and referred to it as African American History Month! The proclamation read:

> As we celebrate National African American History Month, we recognize the heritage and achievements of African Americans. The contributions African Americans have made and continue to make are an integral part of our society, and the history of African Americans exemplifies the resilience and innovative spirit that continues to make our Nation great.

I understand that it can be confusing, especially depending on the timeframe and what is going on in politics at the time, but based on his poor showing among Blacks, Trump knew that the world was watching. If he has any talent, it is his ability to stir up debate with his divisive rhetoric. That's what he did when he purposefully avoided using the word *Black*. People out in the community were upset, asking me what it was about. They understood that either I knew or could find out what was going on. The concern was that this man, who did not have a stellar record with the Black community, was possibly redefining traditions in Black America. Folks were getting angrier by the moment. They said they called me because I had my finger on the pulse of what was going on. However, at that time, I had no clue. The email drew my attention to the problem. I did what I always do; I went looking for answers. I walked to Sean Spicer's office and asked about it. He said that they had been working on the proclamation. I explained that it was not about the proclamation; it was about the naming of the month.

We both went back and did some due diligence. Spicer came back saying, "Well, President Obama called it African American History Month on his proclamations." But what Sean had failed to do was to go way back. I had access to a website that archived every presidential action and proclamation. President Ford had started the February proclamations as Black History Month, but the words were changed during the Reagan years to African American History Month. Someone from the Trump administration had intentionally tried to stir up anger and tension between the Black community and this White House. It was someone who had access to the proclamation. Who could it have been?

Meanwhile, in the press secretary's office, Spicer and I talked about the title. He didn't understand that there was a growing concern about the title of the TMZ online article. In his office, which press secretaries before him had used, he looked up the story, and saw the title and the leaked proclamation. He then called TMZ demanding an answer as to who leaked the story and asked them to change the title of the article. TMZ was said to be upset about being misled on this story. It was someone in the White House who had offered the information and the context. I asked an official from TMZ who it was, and they declined to give the source. But then I got specific and pointedly asked if it was Omarosa, and the person said, "All I can say is it may or may not be, as the entire incident was very ugly."

The next day, there were stories about Omarosa having some sort of "emergency issue," and she was soon spotted wearing a leg brace. (She has a TV history of experiencing illness or injury when faced with opposition, and it always seems to divert the attention. She did so on *The Apprentice* when a piece of sheetrock at a construction site fell, and later on *Celebrity Big Brother* when she lost a competition and came down with an asthma attack.) For that Trump White House incident with her leg, TMZ wrote "Central Casting" into the title of their story as it related to her alleged leg problem. I also tweeted something like "poor baby"! Very soon after, Omarosa was on the rampage for me. Maybe I shouldn't have gone on social media making a joke of her alleged health issue, but after all, she had been telling Sean Spicer not to call on me at the White House press briefings. Spicer had told me that himself, so I was upset by the betrayal of my supposed friend. Also, she had lied about me to a dear Republican friend, saying that I had said something on Twitter about that person, which I had not. That friend knew she was lying because they retweeted my post that was in question.

Laying all of it out now it does seem somewhat silly and inconsequential, and it would be if not for the fact that she was attacking my profession and my character. Her attacks directly affected me and my career and my children. It was not a position I wanted to be in, and trying to extricate myself did not seem to be working. She was determined to have the last word, to show that she had the upper hand, and it was stressful and upsetting.

Omarosa's attempts to smear me with her lies started in the summer of 2016 and continued through 2017. Finally, I'd had enough of it. I asked her, just outside of Sean Spicer's office, why she was telling Sean not to call on me. Think about this: if my questions were stifled, the Black community, which is still hurting, would not have their questions asked. How could she justify that? It was said that part of her role in the White House was to represent the Black community and act as an outreach. I knew that she was not interested in anything like that. She was focused on trying to position herself as best she could to look good in Trump's eyes. If she made him happy, just as she had done on his reality show by bringing the ratings, he would reward her.

She did plenty of vengeful things toward me, but telling the press secretary not to call on me was the most egregious. That meant she was toying with my integrity and my professionalism. She was also attempting to stifle my voice as one of the reporters of the Black community, people she was supposed to represent. That was maddening to me because no matter how desperate someone is for power, jeopardizing an entire community's representation in that briefing room was inexcusable. It's possible that she didn't understand the ramifications of what she was doing, that she was just out to get me, but knowing her, she had thought things out in advance. She knew how she wanted things to go and what the results would be.

When I confronted her, she went into full *Apprentice* mode in less than a second. She was incredibly animated, moving her neck and body, acting a fool. She screamed so loudly I thought she was trying to get the president to come jump in the argument. We were feet from the Oval Office. I could see the door clearly. I was ready for whatever she was putting down and for whoever would join her. It was time to stand up to the mistreatment and deal with it head on, out in the open, whether I was ready for it or not.

That's when the clash got real and threatened to get physical. But before this April and Omarosa verbal showdown, there had been another altercation earlier that day. Mind you, the hate was percolating in the press area of the West Wing. A conservative Black female reporter had openly, in my presence, spoken the wrong words, saying, "The only reason you get called on is because you're Black."

To this day, those words don't sit well with me. At that time, I had had enough! "Yes!" I said to her. "You ain't shit!" in front of everyone, asking her, "Who you think you are? You're Black too, in case you didn't know it!"

I guess she felt "entitled" as she was conservative and thought she could outperform a seasoned reporter who'd been there perhaps since before she was born. Well she quickly figured out: Don't go there again! My words made her cry, and days later she came to me saying Omarosa had wanted the details of what happened between us. (Interestingly enough, since Omarosa's firing, that same reporter has been trying hard to be friendly to me.)

So, that day I was worked up. Back to the real clash, the one with the Honorable Omarosa, who was still wearing a medical boot and moving about on a scooter. We went at it openly, right outside Sean Spicer's office. Our altercation spilled into the hallway between the Oval Office and Sean's office, then back into Sean's outer office. I simply asked Omarosa if I could talk with her and wanted to specifically know why she was telling Sean not to call on me. She then turned the tables and said, "If you were my friend, why would you laugh about me being taken out on a stretcher from the White House?" Mind you, that had been the previous week.

I was just amazed to find myself in this position. With one teenage girl and a preteen, I know how friends can be challenged and the silly fights that can occur. For the life of me, I could not understand exactly how I had gone from conducting myself professionally every day for the past twenty years and suddenly I was fighting for my reputation like a kid in a schoolyard. It was a bizarre situation, but I was now dealing with an administration that seemed to allow just about anything. Maybe this was my new reality.

By that Thanksgiving, any friendship she and I may have had was finally gone. I didn't use any curse words on Omarosa, but the things I said were meant to cut deep. This showdown had been in the making for a while, and now its time had come. She would know that I knew what she was up to and would expose her for the fool and fraud she was.

It felt like my version of the "Hillary" moment in the debate with Trump. This time it was Omarosa circling around me (or more accurately wheeling around me), challenging me, daring me to push back. Like most bullies, she was counting on my professionalism to save her. She thought that I would be afraid to challenge her right there, that I would back down and want to talk later. But that's not what I wanted. I needed it to be out in the open for everyone to hear. I was tired of her secrets and the way she manipulated everything to twist it to her benefit. This time I would not allow her to attack me in the shadows where no one could see or witness and where she could lie about it. This time I was ready.

I knew it was a calculated risk, because I had learned that I never knew which person I was going to get. Would it be the reality villain or the ordained minister or the White House employee? I also wasn't confident that the others at the White House would back me up. None of that mattered, though. This was my "debate moment," and I was going to stand up to the bully. This was my time to be firm and clear that I wouldn't continue to play these games. I was going to do my job and I wasn't going anywhere, no matter what trick she pulled.

When I confronted her, she continued to scream, obviously hoping to bring attention to herself, possibly hoping her boss would come to the rescue. I was prepared for her and didn't let her aggression bother me. She lied, saying that I had said on Twitter that Trump should be impeached. I replied, "Since you're trolling all my social media, prove it." I had tweeted weeks before that a congressional leader had said it would take a little more time for any impeachment proceedings. I was clear in my tweet and she twisted it, saying that I had made the statement, not the member of Congress. Another lie. The issue of the dossiers that were supposedly kept on me during the campaign came up. She also shouted that I was taking money from Hillary Clinton, and I said, "Maybe I should because I hear it's a lot of money." I added, "Girl, at least I have my books and this job, and before you became the honorable scoot-scoot, you were selling cell phone contracts." Yes, it's true. Her representative name was Onee, but I never got the Onee cell phone hook-up. Dang! Those phones are expensive!

Kidding aside, I also firmly remember telling her, "I was here when you were fired the first time, and I'll be here when you get fired this time!" It was not a prediction, but an understanding of what happens with her in most situations. I was aware of the pattern and sure that it would repeat itself. I also told her, "I will never be in your wedding, even after you've begged me."

The verbal sparring match carried on apparently for about twenty minutes, with her or her assistant audio recording the session on her cell phone and many in the press office looking on in shock. One person kept saying, "Come on, ladies," but never intervened. I remember Omarosa saying, "I can't believe this is happening in my office." So I said to her, "Valerie Jarrett wouldn't act like this." (She had prided herself on being this administration's Valerie Jarrett.) That's when she came over to me as I leaned on Sean Spicer's closed office door. She hopped up on her boot and hovered closely over me. I said, "You better back up because this is Secret Serviceable." Then she darted into Sean's office, and she apparently continued to complain about me for most of the afternoon. (I did tell Omarosa during the confrontation and Sean and Reince after the shouting match that if she continued to tell that lie she would be sued.)

A Trump press office staffer, Jessica Ditto, immediately pulled me into her office asking me, "What did Omarosa do to you physically?" She had not seen anything since Omarosa's back had been turned toward her, when Omarosa had hovered over me so no one could see what she was doing.

I told Jessica, "She didn't touch me, but she was totally in my personal space."

Later that evening, Omarosa evidently was not satisfied with what-ever Sean's response was, so she called my boss, Jerry Lopes, at the American Urban Radio Networks (AURN). He told her, "Let me stop you here. April has been telling us everything all along. If you two are truly friends, you would take her out for a drink." According to Jerry, she said, "The boss doesn't like for us to drink!"

Jerry was well aware of all things relating to Omarosa's antics. A few years prior, my network had lost a work contract with talk show host Wendy Williams, which company officials blamed on Omarosa. It all happened when Wendy Williams and her husband, Kevin, were the American Urban Radio Network's guests at the 2010 White House Correspondents' Association Dinner. The two of them had to leave early, hours before the dinner. For some strange reason, after the dinner news reports popped up that the two women, Wendy Williams and Omarosa, had tangled over seating at the dinner, but that was not the case.

Wendy and her husband left, and we still had their two tickets, so since Omarosa and I were friendly at the time I gave one to Omarosa and the other to another woman. Wendy and her husband were never at the dinner for any of what was alleged to have happened. They had left right after the Tammy Haddad Annual Garden Party. Mind you, Wendy had been on the air talking about how excited she was to be going. She said later her allergies had acted up, and she had to leave. Her departure could have also had something to do with a problem I was not privy to with AURN as she was doing an entertainment radio show for them at the time. Jerry and other AURN executives kept sug-gesting it was Omarosa who had planted the lie about her and Wendy fighting over the seats in the media to get the press. I didn't want to believe it. But when Omarosa was fired from the White House (the second time), Jerry asked me if I now believed she had planted that false story years ago about Williams. I said, "Yes!"

Back to my confrontation in the White House with Omarosa. There were Trump staffers around during that confrontation, and there was one reporter who heard a good portion of it. *The Washington Post* got the story, and they had even verified aspects of it with their reporter, Abby Phillip, who was there. Abby acknowledged that she heard me say, "You better back up. This is Secret Serviceable." However, the fact was that I did not want to be the story. Omarosa came to physically intimidate me because I had embarrassed her.

That clash happened a week-and-a-half or so before Trump's first solo press conference, in the East Room of the White House. Before I get to that, let me tell you a bit about press conferences and how they came to be.

There is a long history to these must-watch televised press conferences and briefings. According to the White House Historical Association and Dr. Martha Joynt Kumar, White House briefings began in the 1800s, conducted by the presidential private secretary, a position analogous to the chief of staff today. It was back in 1913 when Woodrow Wilson held the very first press conference, over one hundred years ago! Those press conferences were open to reporters but off the record. Some information was led by reporters, and President Wilson was angry. The next year, the White House Correspondents' Association (WHCA) was formed to support "the interests of those reporters and correspondents assigned to cover the White House." It started because there were rumors that the same reporters were chosen to cover those press conferences and that needed to change. And it did.

Those press conferences became a regular occurrence, and by 1929 President Herbert Hoover hired the first press secretary. Franklin D. Roosevelt held informal press conferences right in the Oval Office and was the first president to use radio to promote his policies. Eleanor Roosevelt was the first First Lady to hold an official press conference, and that continued while her husband was in office.

When Harry Truman was in office, he proposed an expansion of the West Wing that would add a studio where the press briefings could be held. But it did not happen because Congress did not support it, so he chose to hold them in the Indian Treaty Room in what is now the Eisenhower Executive Office Building.

In January 1955, the press secretary of Dwight D. Eisenhower provided equipment to record tape-delayed press conferences for television. Then in 1961, the very first live televised news conference was held by John F. Kennedy. Kennedy held his press conferences at the State Department. The next office holder, Lyndon B. Johnson, changed things considerably by holding press conferences anywhere and at any time he wanted. Another important moment, January 1995, Mike McCurry, then-President Bill Clinton's press secretary, allowed for the White House press briefings to be televised, further promoting White House transparency.

At that first solo Trump press conference I wasn't thinking about my fight with Omarosa at all, but I wanted to know about President Trump's "Black agenda" because he had talked of an inner-city fix on the campaign trail. And after less than a month on the job, President Trump had spoken, and the world watched, listening carefully to his comments on fixing the inner cities.

During that press conference, on February 17, 2017, literally pulled together in forty-five minutes, I asked a few questions of President Trump. Here's a transcript of our exchange:

TRUMP: Go ahead.

RYAN: Mr. Trump?

TRUMP: Yes, oh, this is going to be a bad question, but that's OK.

RYAN: It doesn't have to be a bad question.

TRUMP: Good, because I enjoy watching you on television. Go ahead.

RYAN: Well, thank you so much. Mr. President, I need to find out from you, you said something as it relates to inner cities. That was one of your platforms during your campaign. Now you're—

TRUMP: Fix the inner cities.

RYAN:—president. Fixing the inner cities.

TRUMP: Yep.

RYAN: What will be that fix and your urban agenda as well as your HBCU Executive Order that's coming out this afternoon? See, it wasn't bad, was it?

TRUMP: That was very professional and very good.

RYAN: I'm very professional.

TRUMP: We'll be announcing the order in a little while and I'd rather let the order speak for itself. But it could be something that I think that will be very good for everybody concerned. But we'll talk to you about that after we do the announcement. As far as the inner cities, as you know, I was very strong on the inner cities during the campaign. I think it's probably what got me a much higher percentage of the African American vote than a lot of people thought I was going to get. We did, you know, much higher than people thought I was going to get. And I was honored by that, including the Hispanic vote, which was also much higher.

And by the way, if I might add, including the women's vote, which was much higher than people thought I was going to get. So, we are going to be working very hard on the inner cities, having to do with education, having to do with crime. We're going to try and fix as quickly as possible—you know, it takes a long time.

It's taken more a hundred years and more for some of these places to evolve and they evolved, many of them, very badly. But we're going to be working very hard on health and healthcare, very, very hard on education, and we're going to be working in a stringent way, in a very good way, on crime.

You go to some of these inner-city places and it's so sad when you look at the crime. You have people—and I've seen this, and I've sort of witnessed it—in fact, in two cases I have witnessed it. They lock themselves into apartments, petrified to even leave, in the middle of the day.

They're living in hell. We can't let that happen. So, we're going to be very, very strong. That's a great question and—and it's a—it's a very difficult situation because it's been many, many years. It's been festering for many, many years. But we have places in this country that we have to fix.

We have to help African American people that, for the most part, are stuck there. Hispanic American people. We have Hispanic American people that are in the inner cities and they're living in hell. I mean, you look at the numbers in Chicago. There are two Chicagos, as you know.

There's one Chicago that's incredible, luxurious and all—and safe. There's another Chicago that's worse than almost any of the places in the Middle East that we talk, and that you talk about, every night on the newscasts. So, we're going to do a lot of work on the inner cities.

I have great people lined up to help with the inner cities. OK?

RYAN: Well, when you say the inner cities, are you going—are you going to include the CBC, Mr. President, in your conversations with your—your urban agenda, your inner-city agenda, as well as—

TRUMP: Am I going to include who?

RYAN: Are you going to include the Congressional Black Caucus and the Congressional—

TRUMP: Well, I would. I tell you what, do you want to set up the meeting?

RYAN: Hispanic Caucus—

TRUMP: Do you want to set up the meeting?

RYAN: No—no—no. I'm not—I'm just a reporter!

TRUMP: Are they friends of yours?

RYAN: I'm just a reporter.

TRUMP: Well, then (ph) set up the meeting.

RYAN: I know some of them, but I'm sure they're watching right now.

TRUMP: Let's go set up a meeting. I would love to meet with the Black Caucus. I think it's great, the Congressional Black Caucus. I think it's great. I actually thought I had a meeting with Congressman Cummings and he was all excited. And then he said, well, I can't move, it might be bad for me politically. I can't have that meeting.

I was all set to have the meeting. You know, we called him and called him. And he was all set. I spoke to him on the phone, very nice guy.

RYAN: I hear he wanted that meeting with you as well.

TRUMP: He wanted it, but we called, called, called and can't make a meeting with him. Every day I walk and say I would like to meet with him because I do want to solve the problem. But he probably was told by Schumer or somebody like that, some other lightweight. He was probably told—he was probably told "Don't meet with Trump. It's bad politics."

And that's part of the problem in this country. OK, one more.

Within two hours, the Congressional Black Caucus head, CBC Chairman Cedric Richmond, received a call from the assistant to the president and Black outreach person—Omarosa Manigault. She said she had been trying for months to arrange a meeting, especially when

Trump was president-elect. It had never happened until the hot spotlight of Black issues was front and center, thanks to the president's unique way of emphasizing his concern, dismay, and even anger. I'm not sure what it was that day, but I'm thankful he called on me as issues of urban America were a minimal part of his campaigning for the Oval Office. But getting into the weeds of that strange back and forth with the president, while others say it was sexist and racist, I say it was also part of the sinister influence of Omarosa. I find his words "Aren't they your friends?" to be interesting, since they implied something more than a professional work relationship.

Meanwhile, Congressman Richmond, speaking of President Donald Trump asking me to set up the meeting between him and the Congressional Black Caucus, reflected, "The question is just whether it is intentional, intentionally misinformed or unintentionally misinformed. But definitely the fact that he just doesn't know any better just like it is not your role to set up an interview. But the question becomes why would he say that as if you know us? Because you're Black?"

Things escalated quickly! In March, just weeks later, Sean Spicer told me to stop shaking my head in the briefing room. (You've probably heard about that incident, which I will detail later in this book.) By then I had reached my breaking point after two solid months of attacks. Alexis Simendinger, a reporter whom I respect, said, "We are not the news."

Alexis said it was about the press standards and norms, not a slight on me. I was going to suck it up and keep moving.

However, I said, "They're not going to write my narrative like they've done for others."

An example of how Trump had done just that was how he had twisted the meaning of the actions of Colin Kaepernick and the other NFL players who were "taking a knee" during the national anthem to protest police shootings of Black men and women. President Trump, who had the largest microphone, took the narrative and made sure to interpret the players' actions as something totally different. He believed the players' actions were a sign of disrespect for the military, this country, the flag, and the national anthem. The NFL players' goal was overshadowed. And there was the example I saw early on, how Trump kept saying "Crooked Hillary," and she didn't fight back.

I refused to let that to happen to me. The Hillary Clinton example was painfully etched into my mind. So, I defied the journalistic tradition when it came to "not being the story." When what had occurred between Sean Spicer and me circulated in social media and in the news, I became the story by standing up for myself. But the resulting attention was difficult to handle. I didn't want to continue. Things were getting too stressful and intense. On that gut-wrenching press briefing day, I talked, sometimes tearfully, with several folks. This included relatives like former congressman Edolphus Towns. I heard from former Obama administration officials who checked in on me, like Valerie Jarrett and former Homeland Security head Jeh Johnson. I also heard from President George W. Bush's press secretary, Ari Fleischer. They all knew me not only as someone they once worked with but also as a person, and they were concerned because that moment was so ugly. I was even asked if I thought the president had orchestrated Sean's performance against me. I didn't know about any of that but understanding how the press secretaries all played to their bosses, anything was possible, especially now.

I received calls from people I had worked with in Washington, whom I admired and now called friends. They all said, "No, you can't quit!" I still felt defeated on that late-night ride home to Baltimore. I was trying to figure out how I would make a new living with a new line of work. I was thinking about leaving Washington! I had been doing this job for a long time and worked hard to get where I was, and now every day felt like a struggle. Like I was fighting for my professional life. It was exhausting.

Being a reporter is grueling in and of itself, especially in that White House briefing room. I had faced so many professional challenges before—agitated press secretaries, uncooperative White House officials, and aggressive briefing room reporters. However, no matter how hard things had gotten, it had never been like this. I had never been directly attacked and accused of things. I had never been asked to set up a meeting between elected officials, and I had certainly never been told how to respond. How would anyone think that was acceptable behavior? It was beyond me, and I just couldn't decide what I should do.

Then, just outside of Baltimore, I received a call from Ryan Williams of NBC and of the National Association of Black Journalists. I was so close to home that I had already been imagining turning into the driveway and greeting my kids. I had already visualized myself going to bed and trying to put the horrid chain of events of that day to rest. For some reason, laying it out in my head like that gave me some sense of order. I felt like I had a plan, but what about tomorrow? To my surprise, Ryan said to me, "Did you see the Hillary Clinton tape?"

I said, "No." I had no clue of what he was talking about. He sent me a link on Twitter, and I was shocked. Hillary Clinton had spoken in her first appearance since her presidential run. Her talk included support for me and for Congresswoman Maxine Waters, who had been chided by Bill O'Reilly about her hair, of all things.

That was a watershed moment for me, and I was excited to get that high-powered support. However, I was depleted. Earlier that day I had been demeaned, instructed to not shake my head. Earlier that week I had been considering putting in place major changes in my career, deciding if I would stay at MSNBC or move on to CNN. My TV agent, Tracy Smith Wilkes, had been talking to CNN about the move. By showing his ignorance at the podium, Sean gave me the confirmation that this was the right move to make. And when I learned of Hillary Clinton's support, I said, "I'm moving full steam ahead to see what the end will be!" I needed a change and a shift. I had a plan.

After the "shaking the head" incident, Sean told me on several occasions that I should thank him for getting me that CNN contract as a political analyst. He said it several times behind the scenes and even to my boss, who came in to meet with him as he had in the past with other press secretaries. Sean's constant near-obsession with my move from MSNBC to CNN made me wonder if anything else was going on. I later found out through a credible source that Sean Spicer had asked the head of CNN, Jeff Zucker, for a job as a CNN contributor after Trump became president-elect. Sean allegedly made the request while sitting on the couch in Zucker's office. Needless to say, he didn't get the job. That was a clear signal that Sean didn't have a clue he was going to be working in the Trump administration after the election.

Later, when he became the White House press secretary, the railing and rants against CNN went on the agenda for public consumption. Isn't that interesting? The president and Sean joined in the sport of calling CNN and its journalists, particularly Jim Acosta, "Fake and Very Fake News." There's nothing further from the truth, of course. CNN has always been more than credible, and the White House had a huge problem with CNN for calling out foul when it was warranted.

Well, no matter the cause, Sean thought I had received the CNN position because of the way he treated me and the public response to his anger and, at times, his insipid performances and poor behavior at the podium. After I got that job, he ultimately decided not to call on me with the frequency he once had. It was yet another attempt to slow me down, but I was determined to stay and do my job with renewed vigor.

October 26, 2017, in New York City, at an event at the Women's Media Center, I got my chance to tell Hillary Clinton that she was my inspiration as to how to fight back. And I thanked her for speaking up for me publicly after Sean Spicer condescendingly told me, "Stop shaking your head." I thanked my hero. She stepped in, completely unexpectedly, and lifted my spirits when I thought about ending my twenty-year White House career after months of bullying and unadulterated hatred. It was Secretary Clinton's birthday. She was wearing a medical boot on her foot after a fall while going up a flight of steps in London, on her book tour. Before the event, Huma Abedin excitedly took me upstairs to say hello and speak to Mrs. Clinton.

Surprisingly, tears began to form in my eyes, and I became slightly emotional. I was shocked by my fragile state as flashes of the past year swept over me, and I thought of the magnitude of what was at stake in my life. I told her she didn't have to support me publicly, along with Congresswoman Maxine Waters, but she had. I made this clear with my "Thank you!" Mrs. Clinton said it happened to be the truth, and that I handled the awkward moments with "grace and dignity." She also said I didn't have to thank her. But I did offer thanks to her because, even though she sits on a lofty perch, sometimes people still need to know they are appreciated. I genuinely was grateful for her public statement, which I didn't know she was going to make. She spoke of my "integrity"! How humbling.

However, I also had an intention with my words: I told a shocked Hillary Clinton about the lie being circulated that I was taking money from her campaign. I told her that she had taught me not to ignore the political attacks as they had changed her narrative and she didn't respond to some of the smears against her. Secretary Clinton responded by explaining that she could see what would've happened had she turned around and told candidate Trump to stop following her around on the stage. She gave examples of what she thought her critics from various sectors would have said. She explained overall that she believed she would not have been viewed favorably. I agreed, but the lesson was not lost on me.

I was also not surprised that she had given her strategy so much thought. She is a professional and an experienced politician, so it validated my opinion of her when I heard that she had considered her alternatives. Maybe she was right. There's no doubt the extreme Trump activist would have found a way to turn her actions around on her, no matter what she did. So, it was a matter of taking the approach that she felt worked for her, and I respected that.

After our brief chat and my rendition of "Happy Birthday," the conversation was over, and I was escorted downstairs to the event where I was honored alongside Secretary Clinton, who received the Wonder Woman Award, and Jane Fonda, Ashley Judd, and Maria Hinojosa, a journalist on National Public Radio. That was a magical night to be in that company as I received the She Persisted Award!

After I got the CNN position, over the months that followed people watched me persist as I did not allow the efforts to publicly attack me slow me down or affect my professionalism. I guess that is why and how I became the story. Sean Spicer and the Trump administration started out on an unsustainable course. It began on day one with "the challenge of the numbers." Size matters for this administration. And Sean's very short tenure ended in a blaze of shame. Six months and a day from the start of the new administration, he resigned. Many of us warned him. Heck, I warned him. It was as clear as a freshly washed window.

Spicer was spinning out of control and was his own worst enemy. The person he was when he served at the Republican National Committee was gone. He became almost unrecognizable as a Trump sycophant who looked for approval from what I termed as his "father-boss." It was like an abusive and codependent relationship. Sean performed for the cameras: desiring and needing the president's acceptance. Sean became flip, condescending, and rude, hoping to live up to the expectations of his boss who was just feet away in the Oval Office. He even stopped the daily briefings, saying some of the press was "grandstanding." Actually, it was he who was grandstanding, and it didn't work. The president was not impressed and accepted Sean's resignation after

Anthony Scaramucci was brought in to right the ship. The Scaramucci era lasted ten days.

During my career at the White House, nothing has compared to my experiences in the Trump administration. Nothing collectively, in the three administrations I have covered previously, equates or even comes close. Early in the Trump administration, all the journalists were challenged in different ways by the manic pace and constant churn of the new stories, be they distractions or real issues.

Once Sean Spicer was gone and Scaramucci's ten days were over, the mantle was carried on by the new press secretary who was again fulfilling what her boss wanted: total loyalty to him by discrediting efforts and dismissing anyone who questioned him in any way. Thirty-five-year-old Sarah Huckabee Sanders offered a continuation of the condescending behavior and demeaning comments. I was now used to it. I was not normalizing it, but I understood this was their state of play.

With my renewed energy, I was ready to take on any press secretary the Trump administration trotted out. I was going to continue to be professional. I was going to do my job and try my best to get the answers my community and listeners deserve. A wise White House administration understands how the press can help disseminate an important policy or message, and we work hand-in-hand with them to get the full story and share it with the public. I now realized this administration was not going to change, no matter who stood at the podium. The attitude and aggression would be the same. Bring it on.

What was interesting was that Sarah already knew I was a fighter because she had been within earshot of the back and forth with Omarosa in Sean's office. Isn't that an interesting twist? And like the rest of the country, she had seen me withstand Sean's attempts to discredit me. She must have known in her heart that I was prepared for her. Since Sarah's reign began, I have stopped routinely going upstairs in the West Wing and now only go on rare occasions since I have felt attacked, and I do not know what to expect if I do go up there. This is especially so since the Omarosa encounter. I've stayed clear of everyone except for my time in the briefings and on press pool duty, which I usually give away because I have become more and more concerned for my safety. These folks play for keeps.

In September 2017, I had the honor of cohosting the Congressional Black Caucus Phoenix Awards Dinner with actor Anthony

Anderson. As my luck would have it, Omarosa was there. We spotted each other outside the main room during the dinner portion of the event. She slunk across my path making sure I saw her. *Yes, girl, I see you!* When the program began, Anthony Anderson made mention from the stage that Omarosa was at the event. The entire audience booed loudly. Anthony left me at the microphone where I was standing stunned and dumbfounded. All I could say at the microphone after a pregnant pause and then a room full of laughter was, "Your enemies will be your foot stool, and it is not what they call you but what you answer to."

Before she left the room in shame, Omarosa took to Twitter, on her private account, that folks sent to me later. That night on Twitter, she followed Sean Spicer's lead. She gave herself and the president full credit for my success. *Umm, I think not.* The news reports of the Twitter fight were again a hot topic. But for me, the real issue is that none of them gave me anything but a hard way to go. I think of Oprah and her statement, "Success is when opportunity and preparation meet." I have been in the game too long to let the newbies say they did anything for me.

I worked hard to distance myself from anything Omarosa-related, as her residue is toxic. First, I was over the Omarosa mess, and second, I did not want to support that stereotype—not just of catty women, but catty Black women who can't get along. People like to build up any confrontation between two women as a "catfight" but when men disagree it's "a discussion." I didn't want to play into that. I was ready for it to end.

I worked hard to stay away from any of the traps that were sent my way, and I avoided the verbal darts thrown by some people in the administration. I made it clear to everyone that Omarosa and I were not friends, not even acquaintances at that point, and I was going to mind my business. Usually I just ignored them, not wanting to expend any more energy on the issue.

December 13, 2017, was different because of the news. I was awakened with text messages indicating there was some kind of high drama. And indeed, news of a firing came through loud and clear. Not only had Omarosa angered me, but it looked like many in the White House had been ready for her to go.

That was the morning after the defeat of Roy Moore in Alabama. I had been on the air until 2:00 a.m. with Don Lemon and only had three hours' sleep. The text messages kept coming, and I couldn't ignore them. A high-ranking Republican began his revealing and newsworthy text, saying he had received a text saying, "Mission Accomplished," indicating that they were glad it was over! Maybe now things will be different, or maybe not, who knows? I never delighted in the story, but I said, "God, your word is true." The Bible offers Proverbs 24:17: "Do not rejoice when your enemy falls." The Bible also says in Psalm 23: "I will prepare a table before you in the presence of my enemies and my cup runneth over."

For some reason, people still think it's important to share Omarosa's latest antics with me. Supposedly after General Kelly delivered the news of her firing, she tried to get back into the White House to plead her case with President Trump, accidentally setting off an alarm.

She has now returned to her old stomping grounds of reality TV by appearing on *Celebrity Big Brother*, where I hear each day about the latest thing she has shared in the Big Brother house about her time in another house—the White House. Of course, friends being friends, they are always eager to share with me her latest antics. I did not watch, but information was funneled to me, so I may as well have watched her try to regain public standing and vie for a book contract on that show. It sounds less than amusing. I don't need to watch that because I painfully lived a reality with her. It was a lot!

I'll leave it there and offer this. I'm not going anywhere unless and until I'm ready. Now, on to the next chapter.

· 4 ·

Twitter Trouble

It's of the utmost importance that clear thought and conversation be preeminent in the White House. The president has the power of life and death in his pen and tongue. That sounds morbid, but it's true, and it sounds God-like because it is. With this power comes enormous responsibility. It requires self-control over the spoken and written word, especially in the stratosphere of the all-present and unforgiving social media. Twitter is now our blessing and our curse. Anyone can hide behind an emoji and pontificate on their own cyber soapbox. It's also great for the famous and celebrated to communicate directly with their supporters and fans and even their detractors, without a middle-man. However, for an American president, the leader of the free world, where is the line drawn for appropriate Twitter etiquette?

To demonstrate how new all this is, I recall that when I first started at the White House, President Bill Clinton had a computer but never used it. His vice president, Al Gore, joked that he created the Internet. During the George W. Bush years, emailing became more and more prevalent. However, the White House was still giving the press hand-outs, from schedules and sign-up sheets to proclamations and speeches, on paper. September 11 changed all that. Technology became a must.

Back then, most people, like me, had a flip phone or a beeper. The new craze was the Blackberry; you could text messages. Imagine that! During the tragedy of that day, it turned out that the text-message capability on a Blackberry was the only way people could effectively communicate. Phone systems were overloaded, and very few calls were successfully connected. So, understanding that, everyone in the White House and the press began using Blackberries.

The new president after George Bush was hip to technology. He didn't want to give up his cell phone when he came to the White House. Barack Obama was our first social media president and reached younger people on platforms that offered apps, MySpace, Facebook, Instagram, and YouTube. For reporters, White House information became completely Internet-based. But another information and technological revolution came later. President Trump by-passed his own press shop for Twitter. You decide if that's progress or a problem.

We have begun to count on President Trump's consistent Twitter appearances to gauge his thoughts and mood at any particular time. The Bible offers, "As a man thinketh so is he." Well, in my humble opinion, for President Trump, his tweets are revelations into his thoughts and deeds. As Trump tweeteth, so is he.

This statement is supported by Barack Obama, in an interview he did with His Royal Highness Prince Harry for BBC Radio's *Today Show*. The show aired in December 2017 but was taped in Toronto in September of that year. The former president never used President Trump's name, but it was obvious who he was talking about. If not, his remarks fit Trump's current Twitter habit perfectly.

One of the dangers of the Internet is that people have entirely different realities. They can be cocooned into information that reinforces their current biases. The question has to do with how we harness technology in a way that allows a multiplicity of voices and a diversity of views and doesn't lead to a divide in our society, but instead provides ways of finding common ground.

In the interview with Prince Harry, President Obama spoke from his experience using Twitter. His following was then one of the largest in the world. It's interesting to note, President Obama's Twitter etiquette was not controversial as his successor's has been. And ironically, Obama is still the reigning presidential Twitter champ with millions more followers than the current sitting president and the other former presidents. In December 2017, the count was Obama's more than 97 million compared with President Trump's more than 43 million. And it has been discovered that unlike Obama's followers, almost half of Trump's followers are "fake." In this case, size does matter.

On social media, particularly Twitter, people live out their politics in the best of ways and the worst of ways. It's a perpetual platform for any politician, especially those with a new breed of politics with its mind meld against a majority that will not embrace it. Watching the battles of wills on Twitter is like watching the smackdown on WWF (now WWE). In most cases, these days the political cage matches are led by the @RealDonaldTrump handle. The endless conversation with Trump's base and the rest of the world still leaves jaws dropping. Congressional Black Caucus chair Cedric Richmond says, "The one thing his campaign did was empower bullies, bigots, and fear mongers." Twitter is a vehicle that allows influencers to cut out the middle-man and the press agents to get to the heart of it, right to the people.

To understand Trump's consistently erratic Twitter behavior, we must understand the person who currently occupies the Oval Office and calls 1600 Pennsylvania Avenue home. President Trump is said to be keenly aware of his narcissism. But he felt he could control it and be a president for all people when he became Number 45. This is according to the research of *Washington Post* reporters Marc Fisher and Michael Kranish, the authors of the book *Trump Revealed*. But the question is: on what level does he function as a narcissist, with it being all about him? That he really thinks that he can turn his narcissism on and off like that is mind boggling! Let's understand it's all about him and his drive for the center spotlight. Trump is a man who throws word bombs that create an atmosphere of total chaos. He is fully aware of his words' impact and rarely apologizes for mistakes, misspeaks, or mistweets. President Trump is a disruptor.

He holds himself to the Trump standard. Anyone else must stand in the center of their mess and face public shaming and more. But when it comes to being Donald J. Trump, the standard rules of morals, ethics, and just common decency do not apply. They are actually repelled by him.

President Trump was asked about any regrets for some of his tweets at the joint East Room press conference on March 17, 2017, with German chancellor Angela Merkel. Trump flat out said "no" without batting an eye. Here's the transcript of that moment, at the end of the press conference.

> QUESTION: And by the way, my second question, are there, from time to time, tweets that you regret in hindsight?
> PRESIDENT TRUMP: Very seldom.

QUESTION: Very seldom? So you never would have wished not to have—

PRESIDENT TRUMP: Very seldom. Probably wouldn't be here right now—but very seldom. We have a tremendous group of people that listen, and I can get around the media when the media doesn't tell the truth, so I like that.

This type of behavior has a ripple effect. In a March 24, 2017, a *Boston Globe* article titled "Michael Che of 'Saturday Night Live' Stands by Boston Comment;" the last paragraph of the article reads, partially, "Che said he never apologizes for his language or controversial statements because 'I'm just trying to be more presidential.'"

Even as a joke, that's chilling! We look to the president not only as a political figure but also as a moral leader, even though that belief has been challenged over the years. Our kids are growing up seeing things in this president that contradict good parental guidance, particularly his tweets. The tweets during Trump's campaign alone were cringeworthy and caused many to turn off the TV. And now he's president.

As for minority children, they must not display this kind of behavior. At "Mama's knee" they are taught how destructive this is for them. They will not get a "chance" or any "breaks" if they carry on in the same manner as the president. They're likely to be suspended or expelled from school, starting even at the preschool level. Or worse!

During the Clinton and Bush years, reactions to the behavior of our president weren't on electronic devices with some sort of app. Instead, we saw protests. During the Bush years when we reporters were in the motorcade, as we passed them by we would see people in their cars and on the street giving the president the middle finger. Well, now the middle finger is given on Twitter with the venom of words in 280 characters. President Trump is the number one offender. And a woman who was photographed giving President Trump the finger and after acknowledging it got the boot from her job.

Social media is all-inclusive. It's an individual and, yes, a community-use method of thoughts and efforts. The purpose is often to make ourselves look bigger than who we are. In the past few years, psychologists have warned that this behavior is creating a society that's alienating itself from itself. We get the payoffs from high numbers of "likes," "retweets," and "followers," and even from that coveted blue "verified check" and the "dings" that signify that someone has responded to us. The flip side: it's a lot to take in.

Former congressman J. C. Watts says he was on Facebook for about ten months. He admits he left the popular platform because of "all the drama." He says, "Facebook and Twitter, there are some good parts to them. Facebook is like money . . . it is the people with the money that make it good or bad."

When it comes to Twitter, Watts, a Republican, has similar feelings. "I don't think Twitter is good or bad. Some people aren't adult enough or responsible enough to use it the right way. I am terribly concerned that the president of the United States would use Twitter to fight some personal petty battle against somebody that said something about him that he didn't like. I think personally . . . I do think there is a certain dignity that comes with the office that you act beneath the office of the presidency when you get into Twitter battles with somebody."

Watts, chairman of the JC Watts Companies, offers his thoughts about the American public and the president's use of social media. These could play out in the midterm elections. As he says, "We have surely seen a tornado . . . the boards of the house have been taken apart and thrown up in the air. We'll see where they land and how they land after the next election to see if people repudiate that or if they say we don't see anything wrong with it."

J. C. Watts is right about the power of the people and how it's all about what they decide. But the larger question is: Is Twitter the place where our voices can truly be heard beyond the noise of others? People use social media to make their political points. They are even substituting speaking their truth on Twitter for marching in protest in the streets. Mary Frances Berry, the former head of the U.S. Commission on Civil Rights, addressed the Politics and Prose Black Authors Race Panel discussion on January 15, 2018, saying that the Twitter platform is powerful, but not that powerful. "Some people think social media is a substitute for action. It's not. You have to get out and do something."

I think social media is a good place for like-minded people to share thoughts. It's a great place to inform ourselves. In recent years, it's also become an addictive gathering place. And the president is hooked, no doubt about it. He informs us of his thoughts and even creates new words. He's a television critic who has shown us who he is by what he sends out into cyberspace. We peer into his thinking with every thumb stroke.

Because Donald Trump is hooked, he needs to be careful with his addiction. But he isn't. Now the dynamics of Twitter are amazing. On this ever-changing social media platform, people love you and they hate you at the same time. The trolls come out no matter what. Something harmless can turn into a cyber street fight, with a blood-letting that can spell humiliation, job loss, and even worse.

I've seen this and heard and read about it. But the frontal assault of tribalism landed on my table like the basket of plenty at Thanksgiving. No matter how thankful we are individually, we're separated or strategically carved out because of where we stand and who we stand with on the issues. There is no longer any gray area. It's now all black and white. This "us versus them" tribal mentality was invited in to the game, and now it owns the table. It's all about which side of the table you chose to sit on. I work hard to remain a journalist who looks at the table, gathers information, and asks questions of the players.

This nation has been separated down political lines. The old "give and take" exchanges and the "tug of war" of ideas are gone. People are forming alliances and taking no prisoners. The fight is so bad that a dispute over something so simple as a Thanksgiving pie was almost waged to the death. Before I get into the story, let me say that I'm very mindful of what I say on Twitter. "Piegate" erupted over an alleged food selfie that turned into a death match.

Press Secretary Sarah Huckabee Sanders had tweeted out the message, "I don't cook much these days, but managed this Chocolate Pecan Pie for Thanksgiving at the family farm! 2:40 PM – Nov 23, 2017."

Accompanying the message was what appeared to be a stock photo of a pie. When I saw it, I thought she was showing her sense of humor. If I sent out a picture of something I made, it would look homemade, not like a magazine photo. So, my response caused a smackdown over a holiday pie I didn't give two cents about. That simple chocolate pecan pie became a symbol, with the issue being "truth versus lies" or perceived lies. It started out as a joke, but it went awry. When I tweeted, "Show us the pie on the table," little did I know of the uproar and upset that would follow.

Depending upon which side of the political spectrum you were on, that's how you felt about the pie. If you were GOP, whether you believed she made the pie or not, you wanted to stand with Sarah Huckabee Sanders. And it seems Democrats, and those who didn't like the president, stood on the side of the pie being fake. In all honesty, it wasn't just the fact of the pie looking perfect, it was how it looked perfectly photographed, like a cake in a wedding picture. It appeared to be a commercial photo pie, not one that looked like it came out of an oven in someone's home, no matter how many pies they made. The pie became a symbol for those who felt they were lied to in Huckabee Sanders's daily briefings. Americans believed that we deserved better than a lie.

Here's what happened. The day after Thanksgiving 2017, that Friday, many of us were home just doing nothing special beyond being with family, eating leftovers, and checking out social media. That's what I was doing, just like a large portion of the nation. Then I stumbled upon a photo posted sometime during Thanksgiving Day. It was of a pie. And not just any pie but a chocolate pecan pie, a delicacy for some. The photo was very pretty. It was posted by the White House press secretary, Sarah Huckabee Sanders. This pie wound up being a symbol of Truth and Trust. Had I known what commenting on the pie on Twitter would spark, I wouldn't have done it. It was a joke, pure and simple. However, the climate is so poisonous, and Twitter is a cesspool of that mob mentality. I couldn't win.

The back and forth began, both of us in our corners. We were each ginned up by folks who supported us, who watched the White House briefings. I had forgotten all about it the day after I said it. However, Sarah had not. It was everywhere. Fox News was trotting people out to talk about it, to include her dad, former presidential candidate Mike Huckabee. As we talked about it days and weeks later, I realized she felt worse about it than I had imagined. She said she "baked a pie." That might be true. She may have baked a pie, but I still don't believe she baked the pie that she posted on Twitter. That's my opinion, and I am entitled it. But I do believe she bakes. But really, who cares? Who cares? That year I'd decided not to cook or bake as I have every Thanksgiving since owning my own home. It was entirely too much for me to do after working fifteen-hour days all year. The way this thing snowballed, people's anxieties and frustrations played out in a blend of sugar and some nuts. Looking back on it, it was so bad. "Piegate" shouldn't have gotten that big. She was upset and wrote something on Twitter calling me Fake News. That was it. That was a burn and I replied, "The pie was the symbol and the issue was truth."

There was still a tense atmosphere hanging overhead, and it was interesting both of us were feeling the same way on the same day. How did we get here? That day, Sarah saw me on CNN from the North Lawn of the White House. That day wasn't one of the best days in the press room for her. I had spoken in detail about how bad it was with the press. Sarah, through her government email, "summoned" me to her office, and we had a long talk. But not before I pondered what a meeting could look like with her. The trust was not there on both sides. However, we talked. I mean it was a long talk. The talk resulted in us saying, "Let's have dinner."

But weeks later, Sarah brought in her homemade pies. They were beautiful and aromatic. However, I didn't eat any, but I respectfully and gratefully accepted a whole pie in my hands as a reset for the hard feelings we both felt from our daily televised exchanges. It was rough. As I mentioned, former Arkansas governor Mike Huckabee, Sarah's doting dad, even got in on Piegate on Fox News. It was ugly. Mike Huckabee said, "Don't ever, and I mean don't ever, mess with a southern woman and her homemade pies. It is as dangerous as when you hear a southern woman begin her sentence with 'bless your heart,' it means you're about to be gutted like a deer, you just don't know it."

I was in shock at that as I took it as a veiled threat with a smile on it. I wasn't going to let that upset me, but it was a shock. I wasn't alone in giving the side-eye to those televised statements. However, her father knew her sensitivities. Her feelings were hurt. I didn't understand but respected that. I was sick of it and so over it. By that time, I could not have cared less about any pie and all the hype. I just wanted her to show the pie on the table in a picture with folks enjoying it. It was like we all do during the holidays, the food selfie. My original Twitter comments were tongue-in-cheek. But I felt those who saw my tweet went in hard on Sarah. She had become upset reading my tweets and my responses to other's tweets. Who knew she was very sensitive about her cooking? But in the long run I can respect that.

Not eating the pie was my protest against how poorly I felt I had been treated. This was well before the Christmas party controversy. To catch you up: for the first time in twenty years, I had not been invited to the annual White House Christmas party. It wasn't an accident; I figured it was because the White House had such disdain for me and the questions I had to ask in my reporting. Mind you, I hadn't planned on going to the Christmas party. Early in the year, when Sean Spicer had been White House press secretary, I had decided that. It was my form of silent protest.

I looked to the past and those who used their ability to protest as a means of change. It was like the defiance of the silent and peaceful sit-ins, like at the Greensboro, North Carolina, Woolworth's lunch counter. Those sit-ins, and the sit-ins in other places like Nashville and Baltimore in 1960, forced the Woolworth's chain to stop its racial segregation in its stores. All this was in an effort for Blacks to be treated as first-class citizens. Equality was the cause. My silent protest was me "taking a knee." I love my country along with others who protest now and years ago for equality. Not eating that pie was not about Sarah poisoning it as some may have thought. If you don't like me or I perceive I'm your enemy, I won't eat anything you fix. It was a dual issue for me. I was also "taking a knee" on that pie to show my disgust with how the press has been treated.

One aside about pies. Pecan pie. I love pecan pie. I grew up picking and eating pecans on my grandparents' farm in North Carolina. (Yes, I have southern blood in my spirit too!) That tall, old, thick pecan tree would yield bags and bags of nuts for us to take home and crack. I remember the thick green hull that would give way to a brown shell. Depending on the nuts' ripeness, you could put two nuts in your hand at the same time and crack them against the weight of the other. Now that pecan tree is gone, thanks to the ravages of Hurricane Maria.

Back to Piegate. It had been over since around Christmas. But Sarah and I wanted to have dinner and a reset. At dinner we really talked. Our commonality was that we are parents of beautiful kids. It was also real talk, but respectful and with a few laughs thrown in for good measure. I told her this was about a restart, not for any favors. But during the dinner I reiterated that I wanted an interview with President Trump, like I had with other presidents. I couldn't help myself. I'm a reporter!

I wonder if, and how long, our truce will last. Let's see. I am still going to ask the questions I do. Just weeks following the dinner, I asked the president, "Are you a racist?" I know it did not sit well with the administration. Sarah and I are still working through it. At the time of my writing this book, I was still being called on every now and again at the White House press briefings. I still don't frequent the press office, but I'm there in the briefing room.

On one issue for sure, the White House doesn't understand why I ask the questions I do. But there's a large segment of society that does understand. One huge point that came up at the dinner was about the question of: Does the White House think slavery was wrong? I'm clueless as to how the White House could have been perplexed as to why I asked this question. Well, how about Charlottesville and General Kelly's comments on a compromise to avoid the Civil War? The issue of the war was slavery. Where's the compromise? And why did General Kelly call Robert E. Lee, the general of the Confederate Army, "an honorable man"? The Civil War was waged over slavery and the Confederacy wanted to keep slaves. I wanted answers.

All these questions are common sense, but the Trump White House doesn't see it that way. Again, depending on what side of the spectrum or where in the Twitterverse you sit, you see things a certain way. The problem is that instead of trying to understand one another and trying to respect each other's viewpoint, I find Twitter is the latest battleground and the "last stand" for people in some cases.

Twitter has been the perfect vehicle for the harassment of the press by the president and those who are following his lead. That's a lot of folks. In fact, some of the most memorable attacks against me have come on Twitter. I can also say that some of those harassing attacks came from high-level government officials. I can't believe I'm saying that *I've been harassed by federal personnel.*

One of the biggest attacks was from a Black conservative, a former wedding planner with no housing policy experience turned Housing and Urban Development (HUD) official. This woman, who had planned Eric Trump's wedding, sought me out on social media after I acknowledged on CNN that I was receiving death threats. She began responding negatively to folks who were concerned for me and linking her tweets to me. No doubt, she wanted my acknowledgment. Well, she got more than she bargained for! I had taken it on the chin so many times before, but this was too much. My life and the lives of my loved ones are not a joke! I *went in* and didn't care if she liked it or not.

I was even angrier when she sent her first tweet directed right at me; I wasn't worried so much about being called "Miss Piggy." I was more upset about her lie—that Ms. HUD had called me a "bankrupt blogger." In fact, I've never filed for bankruptcy. You can look that up in the public record. I hate it when people lie.

But I didn't get that upset when I considered the source. This was a person I had never met. And her lie could be checked easily through public documents. What people don't know is that back in college I thought Miss Piggy was fabulous! And that was my chosen nickname. Miss Piggy, the strong female on *The Muppet Show*, took no crap and spoke her mind. If that's the way someone views me, I gladly accept the crown.

So, this woman thought she was really upsetting me and that she had struck a nerve. But it mostly just gave me a chuckle. I'm a reporter, White House correspondent, political analyst, bestselling author of three books, and I have a podcast, and yes, a blog. I'm also a mother of two wonderful girls (who I hope will never replicate her behavior). I am sorry she and her friends have a hard time understanding that someone can be good at more than one thing simultaneously.

Sometimes though, when we throw rocks at people, we need to take a close look at ourselves. None of us have any right calling anyone names unless we're willing to follow Whoopi Goldberg's advice. A few days after the woman's tweet, there was a discussion of "mean tweets" on *The View*, begun by Ana Navarro. When my incident came up, Whoopi said, "Until we walk around with our own mirrors, we should stop doing that."

Typically, I don't go after people, but I did this time. I fired back on Twitter. I'd had about enough of the administration's attacks, all of which had been on public display. And sometimes you have just got to say it and call it out. And I did.

What this attempted outing of me did was to shine a spotlight on her and her lack of integrity and qualifications for her job. That's something no agency wants to happen to one of its "alleged, esteemed" heads. She heads the huge New York and New Jersey offices of HUD, overseeing all federal money for housing there. She went to war with me on Twitter without any armor. That wasn't too bright. She also kept up the administration's attempt to go after the press. Again, not too smart.

So, it was tried, and it wasn't a successful attempt. I was "fat shamed" and called a pig, in yet another effort to humiliate and discredit me in this past year. Whether I am or am not fat, it's never right to make personal attacks unless you're above perfection. And even then, you shouldn't do it. I don't owe anyone any explanations about my looks: my nose, my round face, or anything else; I'm okay with me and I love me!

Meanwhile, I struck a nerve with someone. I didn't know why or how, but I just chalked it up as this new political chorus became disgruntled and hateful of me. After the tweet storm with Ms. HUD/wedding planner, what had I done to this new ensemble of neo-Black Republicans? I've been asking myself that since the first battles began. I think Ms. HUD was avenging Omarosa and was mad about my question, "Mr. President, are you a racist?" By the way, she was in the room when I asked that question. Isn't that interesting?

Battles once private are now very public. I've worked hard on keeping things together and seeing them for what they are. This whole thing caught me off guard, and I hope I won't have to do anything like it again. And I don't accept her apology. She was exposed publicly even as she deleted the tweet. We can agree to disagree on anything; however, some subjects are off limits. Be careful thinking you're so much better than other folks. My credentials are verifiable. It's unfortunate that people sling dirt, not knowing their target and when their resume is thin. From wedding/event planner to HUD official is a huge stretch, even if you think it's justifiable. I just don't get the rationale.

Gutter games are just that. I don't play in the gutter and never will. The next day after the public uproar began, I was privy to some screenshots from the Black GOP chat room that Ms. HUD was a part of. I saw that a woman, whose name I won't mention, said, "Someone had to do it." Another Black Republican posted, "It's time we rise up and be who we are and stop this political correctness." This wasn't about policy. It was a long conversation during work hours to smear me. The chats were not just posted by a single person but by many who approved of this nonsense. I saw their names, and I know who they are. The sad part is that there are many others like them. This clearly isn't politics. This is hate! People usually act out this kind of viciousness on reality shows. (Any particular show come to mind?) Sorry, I don't play these childish loser games.

On the other hand, no matter the Twitter fight or anything else thrown at me, I won't and can't be the Angry Black Woman. Too

much is at stake for the country, and for me, professionally and personally. Again, I say, it's not a game. I'll keep my wits about me as the
arrows fly. If you see me on the street, don't hug me, just pray for me.

The attacks are real!

· 5 ·

Enemy of the People

I need to offer a disclaimer before you start reading this chapter. Just to make this proclamation sounds like I'm on the attack. I'm not looking for a fight even as harsh words and numerous death threats are directed against me. I have respect for the highest office in the land. But this past year, the president of the United States called the mainstream media the "enemy of the American people." I have a right, and it is my profession, to question any U.S. president. It's part of the accountability our Founding Fathers included in the Constitution. I'm a proud reporter, like most, searching for answers and truth. That's all.

The power of the news media is not to be taken lightly. Our questions have helped right wrongs and shape policy. We also expose lies. And yes, sometimes we get it wrong. But unlike some politicians, who get it wrong and don't want to apologize or correct their mistakes, we do. We point out updates, changes, and retractions.

A friend, a wise woman, offered the following to me in an email conversation early in 2018. I was pondering our political landscape, and at the time, Oprah Winfrey was thought to be considering a run for president in 2020. This friend, who knows Oprah and did not want her to run, said, "They love you until you're a threat to the status quo!" In this current political climate, the administration tries to annihilate anyone not considered "with them," and this includes the press. The mainstream press has been painted as a threat for exposing the truth, cracking the facade of the status quo.

For this administration, the winning image must always be fought for and preserved at all cost. If it's questioned or challenged, the administration wages a fierce war against any quest for truth and information.

89

In America, reporting is an honorable profession that dates to colonial times. Back then, like today, people needed information, particularly about what was going on in Britain, in the colonies, as well as on the next farm. They got that information through the earliest newspapers.

However, in America 2018, the process of keeping press freedom intact has devolved. There are glimpses of a Third World or Communist attitude toward our free and independent press. This new era of unconstitutional attack is now led by the very person sworn to uphold the Constitution, the president, along with his willing administration.

Make no mistake, there is never a White House that likes everything reported by journalists. Former Clinton White House press secretary Mike McCurry talked about this. A "friendly adversarial" kind of relationship was initially the norm for the mainstream press corps and the Clinton White House. But little by little, there's been an erosion of that type of relationship. It faded with the "art of the deal" being used to promote "alternate facts" in the Trump administration's smoke-and-mirrors game of deflection.

The Trump White House has escalated the "friendly adversarial" relationship into a fight. Repercussions are certain as the goal posts on press interactions are shifted. This is already happening with some federal, state, and local politicians. We're seeing elements of this shift now. Journalists are body slammed, demeaned, and demonized. During the campaign, there were even T-shirts being sold that said, "Rope. Tree. Journalist. Some assembly required."

The Trump administration's efforts go far beyond harsh words and rhetoric against the Fourth Estate. The president goes out of his way to make it uncomfortable for the press. He calls out "Fake News" when he doesn't like or agree, no matter if the story is accurate.

It's bad! The shift has brought the United Nations to speak out against the administration's attack on press freedoms. An article was published in *The New York Times*, on August 30, 2017, by Nick Cumming-Bruce, titled "U.N. Human Rights Chief Condemns Trump's Attack on Media." The first paragraph delivers the stomach punch of this new, embarrassing conundrum.

> Dateline: GENEVA—The United Nations human rights chief said on Wednesday that President Trump's repeated denunciations of some media outlets as "fake news" could amount to incitement to violence and had potentially dangerous consequences outside the United States.

An example of Trump's denunciations of reporting he doesn't like is the following: at the beginning of his administration, the president called out "fake news" on the Russia investigation as a smear tactic. What is in question, then and now, is whether collusion and obstruction of justice by some of the president's closest allies and even by the president and his family can be proven. Stay tuned for that one! But sometimes I wonder if it's the information being delivered, the person delivering, or both that angers the president so that he offers up the term *fake news*. The word *fake* is sickening to me, but more importantly, it's corrosive.

In January 2018, this president went out of his way to try to make it uncomfortable for the press with his ridiculous "Fakies," his fake news awards. People from the Obama administration said, "It would have been beneath President Obama to do something like that." However, President Trump wanted to validate his Fake News label. Thank God I wasn't on that list! These awards just put further targets on our heads. Where is the care and concern about our safety from the highest office in the land? We have not heard that yet.

If you think this is a joke, look at the Knight Foundation's 2018 report "American Views: Trust, Media and Democracy." Page 30 says, "Conservatives are much more likely than liberals to say, 'fake news' is a serious threat to our Democracy." In 2017, CNN found that the president said "fake news" four hundred times. That adds up to more than once a day.

On December 15, 2016 a Pew Research Journalism and Media report titled "Many Americans Believe Fake News Is Sowing Confusion" stated that a majority of Americans polled found fake news had caused confusion about basic facts. Sixty four percent of those polled said there is "a great deal of confusion"; 24 percent claimed, "some confusion"; and 11 percent said there's "not much/no confusion."

Today, the confusion reflected in the Pew study about basic facts stems from the climate of hate perpetrated by the president, who sets the tone for his followers. He and his administration have called us "fake" and "very fake." Trump has called us the "enemy of the American people." His former chief strategist, Steve Bannon, called us the "opposition party." This disdain and hate for the press goes beyond words, subliminally giving the "okay" for physical attacks. It's juvenile and dangerous. And if it weren't tweeted by the president, it would be viewed as something innocuous. But it's not.

On July 2, 2017, at 8:21 a.m., the president of the United States tweeted a video of a wrestling smackdown with himself taking down a man with the CNN logo covering his face. The question I pose is, "Is the administration serious about its hate of the press?" No matter the answer, this one-sided battle is now synonymous with the antics of reality TV.

Douglas Brinkley, professor of history at Rice University and CNN presidential historian, contends,

> All presidents struggle with media. You have to create a media strategy. Some court them, bring reporters along with them and co-opt them. Donald Trump's view is to humiliate them, destroy them, to make them seem un-American. The whole idea of confusing people with fake news, while he tells lies regularly, is an abomination. I think we are dealing now with a kind of a crisis in the First Amendment. Because recognizing we can take it for granted that we now have a president that is at a full-time war with journalism.

The power of the White House is the backdrop of this unethical and unconstitutional stance. Brinkley proffers,

> The damage was done when Donald Trump said the press was the enemy of the people. It's a deeply anti-American comment he made. It's a disregard for the First Amendment and it puts journalists at risk around the world. It's the kind of language that Donald Trump uses about the press. It's what you get from dictators. What you get from people that are authoritarian: They want to control. In Russia, he seems to admire Putin so much. You get arrested. You get poisoned. You get sent to a gulag if you seem to ask the wrong questions or you're challenging authority. Trump seems to enjoy that kind of press authoritarianism.

For those old enough to remember, this has happened before in American politics. It was at the highest levels, and it did not work out so well for the person wanting to suppress the press. Douglas Brinkley remembers,

It gets back to Richard Nixon and his enemies list and trying to find ways to get the IRS to investigate reporters and find ways to shut them down and intimidate them. I edited the Nixon tapes. On all of those White House tapes you can hear Nixon wanting to destroy Walter Cronkite: That we've gotta rip Cronkite down to make him into nothing so I can get control. In that case the press ended up getting Nixon. Donald Trump is a student of Richard Nixon. He wants an enemies list. He despises the press. He uses his bully pulpit to demean journalism. I have been very worried at rallies when reporters get spit on, called names, are treated in subhuman fashion because they are doing their jobs. It was a great moment to see where Jeff Flake had his profile of courage moment when he gave his speech from the Senate Well about why we are not 1930s Europe where fascism is on the rise and that it is a danger to democracy when the president talks about the press in the reckless unduly way Donald Trump does.

Nixon had something to hide, and it was exposed by brilliant reporting. Such reporting is also unveiling the secrets this administration wants to keep buried. This could be one reason for Trump's war on the press. But there could be another, very simple, reason. One observer, who wishes not to be identified, says,

> This president has the quintessential, ultimate love-hate relationship with the press. He so craves your acceptance and your approval and your praise, that when he doesn't get it he is all the more upset and all the more rejected.

No matter what we call what the president is engaging in, it's dangerous. There are a lot of stories of death threats rolling around this White House toward the press. I happen to be one of those in the press who has received death threats for simply asking questions. The network I work for has fielded some of those threats, and so have I. They've appeared on the company website, on emails, and on phone messages from people who are not in support of anyone asking questions of the president of the United States.

Early on, I told only a few people about the threats, and I made the White House Correspondents' Association aware of them. But what worked best was sending the information I had to the FBI and local police. The White House has a security force, and it turned the threats over to the Secret Service. I had to step up my efforts to protect myself and my family. The toxicity in the atmosphere is at an alarming level, deadly. My close friends and some family found out what was going on. They were very upset over all that happened and all they were finding out about.

So much information leaked out that I received a call the day after my fiftieth birthday from one of my best friends, a former college classmate, Grammy-nominated singer Maysa Leak. Maysa had relayed the troubling information to Stevie Wonder. Stevie called me, very concerned. We talked several times by phone with long conversations about how to deal with these troubling issues. He told me to make sure I understood the seriousness of this, and that I needed to be watchful. I knew what he was saying was so true! Many people have called wanting to help secure my safety and that of my kids.

At first, I wanted to say that all this couldn't be happening because Donald Trump is the president of the United States of America. A president is supposed to be above the fray. But this president has shown he can't help playing juvenile games and wallowing in the dirt. Therefore, seeing all this over the past year, the earlier rationale is interesting, that he hates us because he doesn't get our approval. Because we don't offer that approval he throws the daggers from the bully pulpit, and some people listen and follow his lead. That's the part that's scary.

Martha Joynt Kumar, the director of the White House Transition Team, offers an alternative view:

> People assume because President Trump disparages the press, he stays clear of most national news organizations preferring instead to connect through interviews with Fox News personalities, such as with the hosts of his favorite show, *Fox and Friends*. The reality is quite different. News organizations are central to his publicity strategies and he responds more often to questions posed by mainstream media reporters than he does to the hosts of Fox News shows. He may call news organizations "fake," but he answers their reporters' questions all the same. In his first year in office, he responded on average to at least one question from a reporter almost every weekday. There were 251 non-holiday and weekend days in 2017, and President Trump responded to reporters on 236 occasions during that year. He did only one solo press conference where he stood alone answering questions for 77 minutes, but he routinely answered questions from the pool of White House reporters, most of whom work

for mainstream media organizations. Not only did his 2,514 tweets set the narrative for the day, so too did his responses to reporters' queries.

With the craziness and uncertainty of this White House, the press does a delicate dance that has to be maneuvered just right. Jeff Mason of Reuters was the president of the White House Correspondents' Association (WHCA) from July 2016 to July 2017 and a member of the board for two years prior to that. He worked with the Trump campaign a bit, was fully embedded with the Trump transition team, and then with the Trump White House. He was the president of the association who oversaw the annual White House Correspondents' Association dinner when President Trump made the historic decision not to attend. The association moved on with the dinner and the show without the president. The focus was on the support for the First Amendment and the efforts to uphold it.

In small windows of time—on the campaign trail, during the getting-to-know-you phase, and at events with the new president—there were some very intense moments with his team. Reporters have recalled times where it looked like the crowd at some of his rallies would turn on reporters. You can see it on television, but to be there in that moment had to be scary. There were also concerns about our workspace in the West Wing.

Jeff Mason says of last year, when he was president of the WHCA,

> I lived and breathed the First Amendment in a way I never had before. Because I had never necessarily experienced the need to fight for it. And I think that is one thing that I learned. Even when things are protected by the Constitution and protected by our laws we can't be complacent about them.

During the 2016 campaign, Mason and the WHCA board met with both the Clinton and Trump campaigns. Jeff calls this the "initial outreach." When asked, Mason advised campaign reporters. He contends the association did not step into the fray in a formal way until the transition started. "That began the night of the election." Mason recalls setting up the pool process and ensuring coverage was intact at Trump Tower. All this was at a time when there was concern that the president-elect did not want the press around, neither there, nor in the White House.

Jeff Mason, the WHCA, and many members of the press and the White House press corps saw unprecedented challenges. The challenges included "ensuring the press pool could travel on Air Force One" and making sure the press could stay attached to the president. This situation was in contrast to the Trump campaign where the candidate traveled without the pool on board his private plane. About a week before the president took office, there was a leaked story that the incoming administration was considering kicking the press out of the White House briefing room. A week before the inauguration, Mason says he met with Sean Spicer about the issue. Mason laid out the WHCA's position very emphatically and made clear what would be acceptable and what would not. In the end, they ended up not moving us out of the press room, but the fight is not over by any stretch of the imagination.

JANUARY 15, 2017 STATEMENT
Subject: WHCA statement on meeting with Sean Spicer

On behalf of the White House Correspondents' Association, I met with incoming White House press secretary Sean Spicer today. We had a constructive, nearly 2-hour meeting. We discussed his interest in increasing participation in White House briefings when President-elect Donald Trump takes office. That has sparked his team to consider moving daily briefings out of the White House's James S. Brady Press Briefing Room to a larger facility on the White House complex.

The White House Correspondents' Association has always advocated for increasing access and transparency for the benefit of all news outlets and the public.

I emphasized the importance of the White House press briefing room and noted that it is open to all journalists who seek access now.

I made clear that the WHCA would view it as unacceptable if the incoming administration sought to move White House reporters out of the press work space behind the press briefing room. Access in the West Wing to senior administration officials, including the press secretary, is critical to transparency and to journalists' ability to do their jobs.

Sean agreed to discuss any additional changes that the incoming administration considers with the WHCA ahead of time.

Sean expressed concern that journalists adhere to a high level of decorum at press briefings and press conferences. I made clear that the WHCA would object, always, to a reporter being thrown out of a briefing or press conference.

The WHCA looks forward to having a constructive relationship with the president-elect's press team and to standing up for the rights of a free press to report vigorously on the new administration.

—Jeff Mason, WHCA president

This targeting of reporters hit home for me on Friday, August 11, 2017, through Saturday, August 12. This was a pivotal time for the nation and a blunt blow for me. The Charlottesville, Virginia, White supremacist rally was originally organized as an angry response over a Confederate statue of Robert E. Lee being taken down. But it was more than reminiscent of a past we are still trying to heal from. The news was everywhere. The visuals were ghastly, with flashes of White men—this time without hoods, unlike other times in our history—carrying tiki torches. That weekend was deadly, with one heroic woman killed by a speeding car purposefully meant to murder during the clash between both sides of the equation.

The idea stung like a thousand bee stings that people could walk through the streets at night with torches. It was a reminder of slavery in the South, hooded Klansmen during Reconstruction, Jim Crow racist segregation, and the civil rights era. Then the next day to see the clashes in broad daylight and the deadly car ramming was too much! It all stemmed from hate, from a thrust to continue the respect for the Confederacy. It deteriorated into rage against Black and Jewish Americans. Racial tension was heightening, and it was thick in the air.

That was also a weekend of celebration for me in New Orleans at the National Association of Black Journalists (NABJ) convention. It was the time when the culmination of my thirty-plus years in my profession came together. I was being acknowledged as Journalist of the Year by the NABJ. What a magnificent honor! My children were there with me to witness their mom receive the award, offering to them an example of how decades of hard work paid off.

We celebrated. We toured the city and experienced New Orleans in some of the best ways, including with friends who lived there and with officials of my network. When I was in meetings, friends gladly took my kids to the things New Orleans is famous for, like the beignets (fried dough with powdered sugar) at Café Du Monde. It was their first time in the Crescent City and a magical experience for me to see things through their eyes.

However, the weekend was marred when I was told as soon as I arrived that Omarosa would be there. My mother instinct kicked in, and I decided to avoid the presentation and take my children on a bayou tour to see the alligators in the swamps. We had such a good time! It was hot and rainy, but we saw gators and made memories. I'm grateful that I made that decision to go on the tour with them. It's one of those special times they'll always love and cherish. I didn't want them to be anywhere near what I figured would be a hot mess that day when Omarosa was due to speak. And it was. Her on-stage fight with Ed Gordon made news. Not only did she start a fight with Ed Gordon, but also with Symone Sanders of CNN earlier that day.

Later that evening, after I spoke on a panel about my books, I was with colleagues in an open-air restaurant bar. We sat there enjoying ourselves for hours. After a while, Omarosa came by and sat down only two tables away from us, when many other tables were free. Just another effort to start drama! I'm not sure why I can't seem to escape her. Folks overheard her handler tell her where I was sitting so she could sit close by. Jarrett Hill, then of NBCBlack.com, got a whiff of what was going down and stood up on a rectangular stone highboy to offer up a toast to me that the entire bar took part in. That put to rest any more of Omarosa's attempted shenanigans for that trip. Folks clearly left there knowing she came to start drama with me.

The next night was my big award. I received it from the then-president of the NABJ, Sarah Glover, along with my college classmate Kevin Frazier of *Entertainment Tonight* and Suzanne Malveaux of CNN. I was on such a high, to be honored by my peers for my work. But the high was short-lived. I was awakened by my iPhone buzzing. Emails and texts were popping up everywhere. It was about a reelection campaign ad—I was the only White House correspondent mentioned in an ad that called Democrats and the media "enemies." The ad said, "Donald Trump: Let President Trump Do His Job."

I talked to one reporter, Alexis Simendinger, then of Real Clear Politics, who was incensed. She felt that if they could target me, they could target all of us. It was real, and it was scary. I now had a target on my head, officially. I told my kids to go and take a trip to the mall adjacent to the hotel and hang out. (And what kid doesn't want to hang out at the mall?) They left gleefully! This gave me a chance to process what was going on with this reelection campaign ad the president had approved of. At the end of the ad, the president said, "I approve of this message."

I went into a fetal position on my hotel room bed, afraid for about two hours. Then I bucked up, knowing this is what they wanted: to make me afraid. But what made it worse: it happened the weekend of Charlottesville, when crazies were making public pronouncements against Black and Jewish Americans. A lot of these neo-Nazi types were following the president, and this was just wrong! In the campaign ad, I was among a crowd of very accomplished talk show hosts, but again I was the only person who was a reporter, a White House correspondent. I thought, "I love my country and my job. Why am I an enemy?" I know why, and so do you. The reasons are many, but they all circle around the fact that I don't represent the Trump base and I'm not afraid to ask the real questions that others are too afraid to ask.

This was another episode of targeting, closer than any other. I had received threats before, but an in-person attempt to shut me down and intimidate me was in my face! A few months later, in the new year, the tables were turned on me again during the Martin Luther King Day event in the Roosevelt Room of the White House. I asked the question no reporter has ever asked a sitting U.S. president: "Are you a racist?"

The president ignored my question and that of another reporter. But then I asked: "Will you answer these serious questions?" An obsessed Trump supporter, Darrell Scott, went on the attack. Surprisingly enough, this man was once a prisoner, now turned minister, who boasts a friendship with Donald Trump and has known him for years. This was not about politics as I see it. It was about this Black man from Cleveland standing up for an already larger-than-life figure.

Think of it: this man's connection to power after being on the fringe of society. He went from jail to being a pastor of a large church. And then he rented a huge home, traveled in high circles, and maybe at times stayed in the lavish luxury only a Donald Trump could offer.

And then to be close to the president of the United States. He never had it so good! They say when you travel in Trump fashion, it is unimaginable first class all the way. Well, he certainly went back to his "roots and basics" in the Roosevelt Room that day. This minister didn't understand the rules of decorum and the traditional and constitutionally supported back and forth between the press and the president. So he interfered. As the press entered the room, the other attendees of the event loudly cat-called the press, screaming "Vultures."

That day in the Roosevelt Room was also hard because I had to listen to President Trump talk about Dr. Martin Luther King, one of the greatest individuals to walk this Earth. Dr. King was a man who died for equality. That's what he wanted, and someone took his life for it. After the president spoke, Housing and Urban Development Secretary Dr. Ben Carson spoke. Dr. Carson regaled us about individual liberty and equality as they're inscribed in the Constitution. I remember mouthing some of the words of portions of Dr. Carson's speech that were well known.

Then Dr. King's nephew came to the podium and spoke, but someone was missing. In fact, at least three people were missing. The surviving children of Dr. King were not there. Martin III, Bernice, and Dexter were conspicuously absent. For decades, anything dealing with Dr. King at the White House had Dr. King's children as part of the event. This time they were not there. I wondered if they approved of all this, such as the special proclamation to expand the Martin Luther King Historic Site to a national park. The King family had been trying for years to do this. Then at the final realization of their "dream," where were they? Why weren't they there?

Instead, their cousin, a man who most of us didn't know existed, stood in their place. Dr. King's nephew was now on the national arena stage where Dr. King's children had been before, and for most, they are still the voice of that great man.

So, after the speeches, everyone moved to the table where the president had the proclamation and a pen to sign it. The president held up the document with his signature. And then he stood up, greeted the guests, and shook some hands as he exited the room. I couldn't waste that moment. It was painful, and I was conflicted, but I had to ask. I had to ask because I've benefited from the greatness of Dr. King to be in the White House and question four American presidents.

As the president was turning and shaking hands, I asked if he would apologize for what he said several days prior with his "shithole" comments. I never used the word *shithole* in my question, just *would you apologize for what you said this week*. He didn't respond. Another reporter asked the same kind of question but used the curse word *shithole*, which in fact was as bad as what I had asked. Again, the president didn't respond. It was then that I asked the president, as he was approaching his sycophant Paris Dennard, "Mr. President, are you a racist?" Still no response! I asked another question, "Mr. President, will you answer these serious questions?"

I didn't hear any response from the president, but, as I mentioned, I certainly heard from a Black pastor who is friends with President Trump. Darrell Scott, of Cleveland, immediately screamed out "No" to my question.

I replied, "Sir, I am not talking to you. I'm talking to the president."

He said, "Well I'm talking to you!" This arrogant, loud, overly confident man came up on *my* job and impeded *my* work. I don't go to his place of business and tell him how to preach or even how to keep a congregation happy.

I immediately turned my attention back to the president as I had only a few seconds left before he vacated the room and that historic moment would be lost. I asked again, "Mr. President, are you a racist?" as he walked out the door headed to the Oval Office, never to be seen publicly again in the Roosevelt Room that day.

The Cleveland minister was lingering among the crowd. I said, "Thanks for being the president while I was trying to get President Trump to answer."

Darrell Scott came very close to me and said, "He was not going to answer you." So, as any reporter would, since Scott had such insight into the president, I asked him, "Would you like to talk?"

Scott responded with yet another "No." He was very angry and came closer to me while playing with the cap of a bottle of water. John Roberts of Fox News and I saw this weird bottle thing.

I asked, "So what's the bottle for?"

Scott said, "To salute you." He even did a gesture like bowing before a queen. It was just weird.

I wondered if Scott was so mad that his salute meant that he might try to take his disdain for the press to another level by throwing water at me in the White House. He didn't. But something happened about half an hour later. In the driveway of the White House, Scott told me that I had been rude to the president. I said, "It's the First Amendment and none of your business." It was tense after this exchange of words. He was told by other reporters to offer me some respect. The problem is, people think the rules of engagement have changed. They haven't changed, although the president wants them to. When will it all stop: this escalation of a very dangerous game with the press and the president and the public?

My question must have touched a nerve, because according to *The Washington Examiner*, the video of me asking the question became C-SPAN's most-viewed video of President Trump. At the time I was writing this book, in just three days the video clip had more than 245,000 views on C-SPAN's YouTube channel, surpassing the previous most-viewed Trump video, which was that of his inauguration. (At last check it was over 389,000 views.) Just for a little comparison, their most watched video of Trump, when he entered the GOP convention, garnered over 845,000 views, while their most viewed Obama video was at the WHCA dinner and has over 10 million views.

Since the summer of 2016, I've been hit by a barrage of efforts to discredit me and take me down. Why? I don't have all the answers. No matter the reason, the attacks are a badge of honor as they further signify I am doing something right, my job. But with all this behind me and I am sure more before me, I'll continue to press for information. However, I've gone through very little compared to my fellow reporters who have been in harm's way overseas and even here in the United States. I stand with my fellow journalists who persevere, regardless of the issue or the obstacle. More than ever before, a free press is needed to offer truth and expose what's done in the dark. We're not freedom fighters or in the Resistance, just people who are proud to tell the truth with pen and paper rather than the sword. Please stand with me, with the White House press corps and beyond, to support freedom of the press. The American Civil Liberties Union (ACLU) states on its website:

The press was to serve the governed, not the governors.

—U.S. Supreme Court Justice Hugo Black in *New York Times Co. vs. United States* (1971)

The ACLU website also says, "Freedom of the press." And, "A free media functions as a watchdog that can investigate and report on government wrongdoing."

As we, the working press, are protected by the First Amendment, I approve of this message.

· 6 ·

Examining the Black Agenda

This chapter is defined by the question candidate Donald Trump placed in front of Black America in August 2016: "What do you have to lose?" The short answer offered by more people than just me was: "Everything!" Literally, this is not a roll of the dice, but life or death for us.

When it comes to the Black agenda with presidents over the years, Florida congresswoman Frederica Wilson says it's typically about "education, criminal justice reform, healthcare for children especially, jobs for young people, for people who have lost a skill set, for jobs that are coming into the market now." She and I have also talked about Historically Black Colleges and Universities (HBCUs), about student loans, about Head Start, about Job Corps, job training. About anything that moves the African American people closer to the middle class and tries to close the economic gap, the opportunity gap, and the achievement gap. She believes, "This is not on the table for this president at all."

Congresswoman Wilson furthers the conversation by saying, "I really haven't been able to determine a Black agenda, except one of hate and insults, and ignorant, bombastic behavior. Making sure that a constituency base knows that they don't matter. That is what I have seen as the Black agenda over the last year."

Congresswoman Wilson is not alone in her thoughts of President Trump. Congressman Cedric L. Richmond, the head of the Congressional Black Caucus, also has strong thoughts about the president's Black agenda, saying, "I think he is misinformed and the question is whether it is just intentionally misinformed or unintentionally misinformed." He cites the examples of Trump's family's past admission of housing discrimination in New York and the case of the Central Park Five, which I described in chapter 1.

Black America has been on the receiving end of hurt and dysfunction stemming from systemic racism in the country since we were brought here in the bottoms of ships. This is not feeling, but fact! The overarching question is: What is the mindset to even put that query ("What do you have to lose?") in front of Black America, who in 2017 and 2018 still have the highest numbers of negatives in almost every category?

And 2017 was the year the White House did not participate in any of the major Black civil rights conventions. In Baltimore, there was the NAACP convention, and in St. Louis, the National Urban League convention immediately followed. Typically, each convention has presidents, high-ranking White House occupants, and other politicians to address the conventioneers. The NAACP convention is usually one of the most sought-after events. In the past twenty years, sitting presidents Bill Clinton, George W. Bush, and Barack Obama have all addressed the crowd. Republican presidential candidates Mitt Romney and John McCain have spoken to the mostly Black audience as well.

Even Governor George Wallace, who said in his 1963 inauguration address, "segregation now, segregation tomorrow, segregation forever," addressed the NAACP. Wallace made a drastic switch in his later years. In the 1980s he asked for the forgiveness of civil rights leaders for his actions to keep segregation alive.

But Donald Trump, as a candidate and then as president of the United States of America, snubbed requests to appear before the NAACP. The civil rights organization had to hear that the president would not attend through the White House daily press briefing. The National Urban League in 2017 did not make a similar request because its focus was on a self-reliant strategy, minus the government in our racially challenged climate.

During the campaign, Donald John Trump had the audacity to hope for the Black vote by injecting that verbal insult ("What do you have to lose?") into our communities, which do not see the world through his elite, Ivy League-educated, billionaire business mogul eyes. What was the mindset of Mr. Trump to even think to ask that inane question with the stakes so high? Do the numbers! Do the numbers in education on graduation and expulsion rates. Do the numbers on criminal justice and on sentencing. Do the numbers on housing foreclosures. Do the numbers in employment on areas of underemployment and unemployment. And do the numbers in health with disparities compared with other American groups.

The answer, I think, is found in something former First Lady Michelle Obama offered during the 2012 election cycle. She said, "Being president doesn't change who you are. It reveals who you are." And during the 2016 campaign, I often recalled the words of the beloved poet Maya Angelou, who said, "When someone shows you who they are, believe them the first time." Harkening back to both of these profound comments, I indeed believed what I saw.

Therefore, the question of "Who is Donald Trump?" begs an answer when it comes to the Black agenda. After covering the White House for two decades, I realize that one president can either help move the rushing tide of change in the right direction or move drastically in the wrong direction. Even though one president will not be able to completely change the hundreds of years of corrective movement in four or eight years, it is far from clear how this president will attack the challenges.

By now, I've been sitting and watching President Trump for more than a year. They've tried to dress him up and have even gotten mad when I've questioned them about certain issues. But his policies come in direct conflict with the efforts to lift the Black community to its best self, a community still searching for first-class citizenship. That status was *marched for* during the civil rights movement and *hoped for* by the slaves. For hundreds of years it has been *fought for*, yet still has not been realized in 2018.

December 6, 2017, I attended the Jack Kemp Foundation event, in Washington, D.C., where Vice President Mike Pence was the main speaker. There, I met with a group of thoughtful conservatives who understood the issues of race and poverty that are still plaguing this nation. We have forgotten about "the least of these," the poorest of the poor, from Appalachia, White America, to the rural and inner-city Black and Brown people.

That night, at the Andrew Mellon Auditorium, South Carolina Republican senator Tim Scott offered that harsh number of "52,000,000" people living in distressed areas in the United States of America. That is a large number of people, too large to ignore. Also, that same night, in a one-on-one conversation with his wife standing by, Oklahoma Republican senator James Langford said it's about the "heart." I will add that if the heart and mind don't line up, we are in trouble. According to the Bible, Proverbs 23:7, "As a man thinketh so is he." We have many laws, but there are still huge problems that have yet to be surmounted. So, Langford is right; it's about the heart.

In that first year of the Trump administration, the Black agenda, with its customary minority issues—the search for equity and inclusion—was not on the table. The year ended with nothing substantive for Black America. The president was remiss, but he had no qualms about going after some high-powered African Americans: CEO Kenneth Frazier, Representative Frederica Wilson, Representative Maxine Walters, Susan Rice, and former NFL player Colin Kaepernick, to name a few. And then there was the so-called tax reform, which will shift massive amounts of money to the 1 percent and may result in a tearing down of Obamacare.

Is anything wrong with working to strengthen a still-suffering community? It was the year the NAACP expanded its tax-filing status because the fight for parity had changed. The nation's oldest civil rights organization needed new tools to work it all out. Issues came to the forefront that caused more angst than any efforts to calm or soothe our hurt community. The Trump White House riled up tensions with the Historically Black Colleges and Universities. The HBCUs were asked to write a list of items they needed for their schools. They were ultimately told that it "may be" unconstitutional to help them.

There was the issue of "taking a knee" because of something Trump skillfully crafted to look totally different than the original meaning or intent. Soon after that, there was the Nazi-style march and murder in Charlottesville. This exposed a deep chasm between the Black community in its fight against White supremacy and the Trump administration.

Congresswoman Frederica Wilson was singled out because she knew what happened to a young African American marine who died in Niger, Africa. And the Children's Health Insurance Program (CHIP) was dismantled. CHIP is the low-cost health coverage in some states for children in families that earn too much money to qualify for Medicaid but too little to have their own private insurance. CHIP also covers pregnant women.

The first week of February 2017 was significant for the new Trump administration that was just days old. The administration wanted to change the perception when it came to Black America. What did Black America perceive? The lack of understanding and desire to significantly change the plight of that portion of America not considered "Trump Land." President Trump proceeded to host a listening session with some Black leaders that was attended by a mix of familiar and not-so-familiar faces. Included in this intimate session was a husband and wife pastoral team from Cleveland, Ohio. This religious duo had declared that their relationship with President Trump dated back some years. However, no matter how they represented their religion, they swung their words like a baseball bat. Pastor Darrell Scott and his wife were clear in their disdain for President Barack Obama. They had not supported the efforts of the former president when it came to reducing gang violence in places like Chicago. Trump has often cited Chicago as an example of rampant crime. Darrell Scott even told President Trump in the Roosevelt Room of the White House that the gang members of Chicago had no faith in the previous president and were waiting on him!

As of a year and some months later, the Chicago gangs Scott spoke of were still waiting. No matter if this was a truth or a lie, the finger pointing is strong. However, the overarching issue is: Who is helped by this blame game? Years ago, a Bill Clinton staffer told me something that stuck and has been my gauge for whether a person is there for the people or for power. She said, "True power and proximity to power is about helping people." Pastor Scott's strong statements made me reassess the situation in Chicago. Was it about helping or just talk for the news cameras?

It was just days after the Obama administration had ended, and Darrell Scott's words were a sharp dagger against President Obama, a native of Chicago. I checked in on that city. The ongoing efforts to quell violence in the Windy City were real! The Black community in Chicago wants to cut into the current "gang state" like many of the major cities in this nation. But Chicago was in the White House, the white-hot spotlight, because it is the former president's home. Father Michael Pfleger works with Chicago gangs on a regular basis, meeting with gang members every Monday night. Pfleger believes Scott's statements were all for show. Meanwhile, not long after Pastor Scott's public remarks, his congregation began shedding members because of his and his wife's declaration of unwavering support for Number 45. Father Pfleger said the so-called Cleveland pastor was a joke.

Chicago's Father Pfleger of St. Sabina Church contends, "The poor are dying in our streets. We have abandoned the poor and the disenfranchised in this country. If we don't care for them, the whole thing called 'church' is mockery!" He reminds us of those in the United States who are suffering in the grip of poverty: these people feel "hopeless, they feel forgotten, disposable and that nobody cares."

Father Pfleger says that if he had a chance to speak to President Trump, he would tell him, "If you want to do something to really make a difference in this country, go to all the Third World countries of the West and South sides of Chicago, in New York and Philly and decide you are going to level the playing field. You are going to bring in the jobs, the opportunities, the options. You are going to tell that incarcerated young man, 'You paid your dues. You are going to get a job, and we are going to hire you.' And companies, 'Open up your doors 'cause you cannot discriminate because someone has a record anymore.' Really change the landscape where the South Side and the West Side look like the North Side, and the opportunities and the access are there. Change the education system. Come in and say you may not do it all but you're going to spend the next four years doing as much as you can to equal the playing field, and you will be a good president."

Since that February 2017 Black History Month listening session, Father Pfleger has sent at least three letters to the White House, asking the president for help with Chicago. As of March 15, 2018, Father Pfleger has not received a response from the president or his staff.

Father Pfleger has an offer, if Washington wants to help: "If you want to listen to brothers from the blocks, which numbers about three hundred organizations, you need to talk with people who are presently working with them in Chicago." He says, "If you are not going to follow up with resources and action, it's a waste of time. My first-graders know the problems; we're 'town halled' out. What we need is the courage to now act!"

The Father meets with gang members every Monday at his parish, working to keep the peace. Chicago has been embattled with gang and gun violence, and Trump has continued to call the city out for a fix. Reports indicate that in 2017 the city of Chicago had more murders than New York City and Los Angeles combined that year. Overall, the city of Chicago ended the year with 15 percent fewer homicides than in 2016. That's a drop of about one hundred murders. Chicago saw 664 murders in 2017. And that rate mirrors the numbers of the killings in the 1980s and 1990s associated with drug violence. In 2016 the city logged 781 homicides, and this was the city's deadliest year in twenty years. The irony is that at the end of the year, Chicago police statistics showed the number of people shot in the city was down too: 3,457 shootings for 2017. Yet the murder rate is the highest of any city in the nation.

Father Pfleger contends, "The president's call for law and order as the response to the violence demonstrates how out of touch he is with the roots of the problem. Until we have the courage to get to the roots of the problem ([as with] cancer), it will continue to kill us. If you lock the lions in a cage and don't feed them, one will kill the other if you cage in whole communities with no jobs, schools, resources, etc. We should not be surprised at the violence."

Different approaches could be the reason for the reduction of homicides in Chicago. Remember at that first solo February East Room press conference, the president discussed Chicago as one of his urban fix issues.

Other cities, like my own Baltimore, are also mosh pits of problems, like gangs that some people think are driving up their murder numbers. The year 2017 ended in Baltimore with 343 murders, up from 318 in 2016. But a source inside the Baltimore City Police Department says, "Many people think gangs are the driving force, but it's much more than that. It's drugs, it's accessibility to guns." In 2016, internal numbers show there were no gang-motivated murders, but of the 343 homicides, 295 were done with a handgun and 220 happened on the streets.

In any urban agenda, anti-crime inner-city policing is a part of the fix. Community policing also has an impact, with police walking the beat and knowing the neighborhood. However, in July 2017, President Trump delivered a law-and-order speech that raised eyebrows when he spoke of immigration and the MS-13 gangs. He said, "When you see these thugs being thrown into the back of the paddy wagon, you just see them thrown in, rough. I said, 'please don't be too nice.' Like when you guys put somebody in the car and you're protecting their head, you know, the way you put their hand over, like don't hit their head and they've just killed somebody. Don't hit their head. I said, 'You can take the hand away, OK?'"

Whatever the president was doing, being sarcastic or joking, he drew the ire of policing organizations, but he did receive the applause of the crowd after the speech. That was a cringeworthy moment. The president saw nothing wrong with what he said, but it escalated tensions, particularly of those who did not support his run for president. Let me harken back to a statement made by the Obama administration Homeland Security head Jeh Johnson. Johnson said,

> When there is tension between the community and police, it is a National Security issue. Why? Because the trust is broken and neither side can rely on one another. The example is: "If you see something say something." If the community is scared and/or not trusting, they will not talk and vice versa.

Policing is still an issue in 2018. This year marks the fiftieth anniversary of the Kerner Commission Report. In 1967, President Lyndon Baines Johnson commissioned an eleven-member panel to investigate the causes of the race riots in various cities like Detroit and Newark after police abuse. The report found, "Our nation is moving toward two societies, One Black, One White—Separate and Unequal."

In 2016, Fredrika Newton, the widow of the late activist Huey P. Newton, cofounder of the Black Panther Party, contended,

> It's been fifty years since the Black Panther Party was created in Oakland, California, where police violence and misconduct against Blacks, for decades, went unchecked. Young Black men and women coalesced around the need to stand up, stand down, and stand up for their civil rights in the name of self-defense, hence the Black Panther Party for Self-Defense was born. Despite the tremendous strides in the name of Black liberation made by these men and women, police violence against us has not abated. Today, we see murderous police officers acquitted and set free, one after the next. We all must continue to protest police misconduct, and blatant murder. We must carry the spirit of the Party into the present. Our voices in protest are needed as much as ever.

Here's another negative on this issue, according to Cornell Brooks, the former national president of the NAACP, "You do have a White House that has put the brakes on the use of consent decrees with respect to overseeing police departments that have engaged in police brutality."

In all truth, part of the Black agenda involves criminal justice and policing, and these issues have plagued the Black community since Africans were brought to this country hundreds of years ago. Bad policing must be weeded out for any change to take place. There are active calls to eliminate the residue of some of the ugly police events that lingers. The case of Eric Garner is one of those cases that begs for closure. He was the Black man who died in a police chokehold in New York City. Garner's death was caught on multiple cell phone cameras.

The family and witnesses contradict what the police have told the nation, which was that he was selling loose cigarettes at the time of his death. His mother, Gwen Carr, says her son had broken up a fight at that spot where he died, and he was the last one there when the police arrived. They charged in, taking him down, maybe believing he was part of the altercation. Garner was placed in a chokehold, and he called out eleven times, "I can't breathe!" He was telling the truth. According to his mom, he had a history of respiratory issues, asthma. He died at the scene.

Eric Garner's mother continues to search for justice for her son. Prior to President Obama leaving office, the Justice Department was well aware of the unique nature of the case. New lead investigators in the case are now on the job because there was a deadlock with the original investigation team on whether to indict the officer or officers involved in Eric Garner's death. Within the first one hundred days of the Trump administration, Mrs. Carr took her search for justice right to the White House. On March 22, 2017, she met with the special assistant to President Trump, Omarosa Manigault. That day Manigault had tried to bring Mrs. Carr into the White House. Those attempts didn't work. So the two women met at Cosi, a restaurant across the street from the White House.

They met, and Manigault is said to have placed a call to the Justice Department, to the Civil Rights Division and then to the Criminal Division, looking for the case to be reviewed. In the past, the White House did not generally directly contact the Justice Department about such matters. But the new attorney general, Jeff Sessions, did not change or set the directive for the Trump administration for a continuance of the rule barring the separation of the White House and the Justice Department. When all is said and done, the Eric Garner case is still on the books, with no conclusion. It is said to be an active investigation.

Former Justice Department sources contend there should be an indict-ment in this case.

On March 22, 2017, the Congressional Black Caucus (CBC) meeting took place in the Cabinet Room in the West Wing of the White House. This group represents 78 million Americans, with 17 million of them being African Americans. Their top five issues were hovering overhead: criminal justice; economic opportunity, expanding the economic pie for minority businesses; education and job training; real crime; and healthcare.

CBC chairperson Cedric Richmond often jokes in public that I'm his "assistant." And if it weren't for me, and my question at that first solo press conference for Donald John Trump, the CBC wouldn't have been waiting for a meeting with the president. What's interesting: the Trump transition team had been working on such a meeting but for some reason couldn't pull it off until the spotlighting of the CBC at that East Room press conference.

Well, the meeting happened, and it was a huge public event. The Caucus members present were Congressman Cedric Richmond, Con-gressman James Clyburn, Congressman Andre Carson (a former police officer), Congresswoman Karen Bass, Congressman Anthony Brown, Congresswoman Brenda Lawrence, and Congresswoman Gwen Moore. They came to the White House armed for informational battle with a 130-page document titled *We Have a Lot to Lose*. Richmond said the presentation to the president was a "business document."

I remember being in the White House correspondents pool that day, representing radio networks. I had to be in the room, and I asked the question that ultimately pulled both sides together. I remember viv-idly, as if it were yesterday, Vice President Pence making sure he made eye contact with me and nodding and smiling at me. That was the one and only time I communicated with him in any way that year.

The Congressional Black Caucus and the president stayed in the Cabinet Room for a long time. But Congressman Richmond contends the president didn't read their book of responses to his campaign ques-tion, "What do you have to lose?" The president didn't read it, nor did he respond to it. But Cedric Richmond says there was a "take away" or a lesson learned from the meeting that was surprising. He says Trump was more into getting to know the Black leaders than their efforts on policy. He says,

I think I am an optimist and some people may say I am naïve, but I generally think Donald Trump wanted to have a relationship with the African American Caucus, the Black Caucus. But I don't think it was based around policy and doing anything for the African American community. I think it was all based on him wanting some friends, some social type friends because that is where the conversation was headed, nine out of ten times, until we directed it back. I think he was genuine in his desire to have a friendship, but I don't think that friendship was going to have anything to do with policy. I think it would have just been, "Hey you guys want to come over to bowl at the White House or have drinks or something?" And that we just can't afford to do right now, if ever.

Just months into this new presidency, President Trump wanted to emblazon that moment in history with pictures of Black people standing behind him at his desk with smiles on their faces. The Congressional Black Caucus leaders didn't want that. They remembered what had happened with the Historically Black Colleges and University presidents. They were not happy at all. The president asked them for a picture, but the Congressional Black Caucus said the only way they would take an Oval Office picture was if it was a photo of them sitting and working, not standing and smiling behind the president's desk. So, what exists is a picture of the CBC engaged in conversation with the president by the fireplace in the Oval Office. About the meeting, Congressman Richmond said, "We covered it all! We covered everything from Rural America to Flint [Michigan] to the HBCUs to the budget and infrastructure, including broadband and water systems. We talked about public education. We talked about public housing. We talked about healthcare."

What was also important during the meeting was that both sides, the president and the Congressional Black Caucus, challenged each other about their rhetoric both during the campaign and after Trump became president. Each side had used their words strategically against each other, from the presidential campaign until the meeting. At the meeting, the CBC wanted resolution of, or at least some work toward, fixing the problems detailed in their booklet. They also wanted to deal with the president's problem of his knee-jerk reactions. So, the two sides faced off about their caustic words. A source says when asked by the CBC to stop, the president never said he would stop his hurtful statements. The president also told them about what he felt were harsh words from the CBC, and the CBC never said they would stop the verbiage either. The stalemate was evident on the strong issue of divisive rhetoric.

At the end of the meeting, when the CBC members met with the press, one of the last questions that March day was a query about whether the members thought the president was a racist. Membership head Cedric Richmond said, "You would have to ask those who are posing the question." Months later, that answer would drastically change for many Black leaders, including a large portion of the membership of the Congressional Black Caucus.

However, there was a promise at the meeting: the Trump administration said it would have the members of the Congressional Black Caucus meet with cabinet officials to discuss every area of concern on the CBC list affecting CBC constituents. Those meetings and calls never took place! And then when the invitation came for a second meeting with the president, CBC officials said, "No!"

Another reason for the CBC's refusal to meet again was that the person considered the "Black minder" (the person conducting Black outreach) at the White House continued to taunt the head of the CBC, working to undermine him among the members of the Caucus and other Black leaders. Congressman Richmond had enough class not to respond. What is interesting is that the then-White House staffer found time to pick a fight with the Black membership of Congress but never had the time to follow through on any of the promises of the first CBC meeting, and then expected another meeting. That was asinine!

That was not the last attack on a member of the CBC. The week of October 16, another member—Congresswoman Frederica Wilson— was in the bullseye of a verbal assault to diminish and discredit her standing and truth. It stemmed from a devastating and sorrowful event that gripped the nation: the death of four American soldiers in October 2017.

Sgt. La David Johnson, Staff Sgt. Bryan Black, Staff Sgt. Jeremiah Johnson, and Staff Sgt. Dustin Wright were killed when they were ambushed in a surprise attack in Niger after inaccurate intelligence was given to them. The men had received the okay to travel to Niger to help support soldiers who were trying to stand up against terrorist groups there like Boko Haram. After the soldiers' deaths, Miami congresswoman Wilson noted that the group was not properly armed, nor were they in armored vehicles when they were subjected to a fierce attack.

Congresswoman Wilson was getting rapid information about the attack because of her political connections with Army Intelligence, because of her closeness to the family, and because of her work on finding the missing and kidnapped Nigerian girls. She was considered "family" of one of the fallen, Sgt. La David Johnson. Frederica Wilson felt the Johnson family's innermost anguish. And she knew of the family's plans as they transpired. She even knew why and when the family questioned the government, particularly the military, and about what was missing from Sgt. Johnson's casket.

In January 2018, during the phone interview for this book, months after the funeral for Sgt. Johnson, the congresswoman acknowledged that the sergeant's body was in the casket but his widow had received his teeth after he was laid to rest. Congresswoman Wilson said La David's teeth were allegedly found in Niger, "knocked out" of his mouth. The body was laid to rest, but the family has Sgt. Johnson's teeth in their personal possession.

This information lends credence to the reports that there was indeed an attack, but the questions still loom as to what happened. Congresswoman Wilson was in the car with the Johnson family as they were going to the airport to meet the body of their son, husband, and friend. That seems normal, especially since she had known the deceased since his childhood and was considered family.

A master sergeant was in the car along with the congresswoman and the widow and parents of the fallen solider. It was the master sergeant who took the call from the president and played it on speakerphone for the family to hear along with the congresswoman. At the very least, the family was disappointed with the president's conversation. He allegedly forgot Sgt. La David's name by repeatedly saying "your guy." They also felt it was in poor taste for the president to share his sympathies and in the same breath say, "He knew what he signed up for."

So, how and why did the president's words come out wrong at a time of great grief? The moment was hard, and the president, who has been accused of lacking empathy and a true sympathetic nature, was shocked by the dismay and public burn by the revelation of the conversation. Everyone was talking about this hurt-filled moment. People kept re-creating their own version of how it should have gone to make the series of painful events bearable, if that were possible.

What do you say to a grieving family in a time like this? I stumbled upon some astonishing answers. I reached out to former Obama administration Department of Homeland Security head Jeh Johnson. He told me that he had been in that tough situation several times. He'd had to inform families of their loss and stand with them to comfort them in the Dignified Transfer as their soldiers "came home." He remembers being there on the government's behalf, by phone or by physical presence, for a coast guardsman, an air marine, and a border patrol agent.

One of those times was when he was at the hangar to meet the bodies of five marines slain in Afghanistan. Johnson understood all too well the pain of the moment. He wanted to respect the families' private grieving process, but also to salute the valor of the marines. He pondered what to say to the families. So, before he traveled to the air force base at Dover, Delaware, he asked four-star general James Cartwright, "What do you say to a family in this situation?"

General Cartwright understood the magnitude of the situation for those receiving the U.S. government's condolences and consoling. He said of a grieving Gold Star family, "They're not going to remember anything you tell them because they are so distraught. There isn't anything you can say that can really help. So, the best thing you can say is, 'You will always be part of our family. We will always be there for you if you need us.'"

Secretary Johnson remembers, "At Dover, it's obviously a very emotional moment for the families who were there because it's the first time they're seeing, live, the casket. There is no ceremony. It is just literally: the casket comes off the back of the plane into the truck and then over to the medical examiner. And the family is there to witness this."

At that time, Secretary Johnson didn't know any of the family members of the fallen soldiers he was there for. But it turned out that the father of one marine, whose body lay "in the back of a C-17," was General John Kelly, who Secretary Johnson would later "applaud the appointment of his successor" to be head of Homeland Security. There were a lot of people there to receive twenty-nine-year-old Marine Second Lieutenant Robert M. Kelly. The younger Kelly died while supporting Operation Enduring Freedom. Lieutenant Kelly was killed during combat operations in Helmand Province, Afghanistan.

Secretary Johnson also remembers that General Cartwright was there at Dover, as was Joe Dunford (assistant commandant), who was the number two in the U.S. Marine Corps, and that "they were there for John."

I witnessed one of those transfers during the Obama years. I was on White House correspondents pool duty, and I watched the bodies of the four U.S. diplomats come home from the deadly uprising in Benghazi, Libya. It was at Joint Base Andrews, in Maryland. President Obama spoke, and so did Secretary of State Hillary Clinton. Also on hand were General Colin Powell and a hangar full of people. I'll never forget the reverence and silence as the flag-draped coffins were taken off the plane and each one meticulously placed in its own hearse.

The death of a loved one is hard; however, the pain is magnified and even, in a sense, glorified, when that person has died in service to this country, laying down their life for our freedoms. These soldiers are heroes.

The irony about this piece of the story is that Secretary Johnson's appearance in 2010 at Dover for that Dignified Transfer came full circle. On November 22, 2016, Jeh Johnson met up with General John Kelly at Arlington National Cemetery over the tombstone of Marine Second Lieutenant Robert Kelly. The pair met on the anniversary of Robert Kelly's burial there. The two men discussed General Kelly's taking over the job as secretary of Homeland Security. Johnson said, "We talked about him taking the job, over his son's tombstone." During the interview for this book, Johnson said, "I was very, very supportive of him coming to Homeland Security."

Because of his loss, General John Kelly knew all too well how this played out for the families. Jeh Johnson believed that when the president heard about what happened with Sgt. La David Johnson, he didn't know what to say and may have enlisted the help of General Kelly. But as the words were delivered by the president, they were hard to hear but impossible to ignore.

A shocking war of words ensued after reporters at the Miami airport asked the congresswoman what the president had said. She told them what she heard, and then the White House shot back, essentially accusing her of eavesdropping. General Kelly, from the White House podium, attacked Congresswoman Wilson's credibility, calling her an "empty barrel," which still haunts her. Wilson says, "He insulted me using a racial term. And it was explained to me that when you call someone an 'empty barrel,' this is a term that emanated in slavery and that is what they called Black people during slavery."

The controversy deteriorated into a war of words, a he-said-she-said, over what the congresswoman allegedly had said at an event that, she notes, the general "was not even present" for. General Kelly and the White House reported that Congresswoman Wilson made remarks off camera about how she made then-President Obama fund an FBI building. When video tapes of that event were released, Congresswoman Wilson said, "*The Sun Sentinel* produced a recording of the entire event to clarify what actually happened, and General Kelly was not there and what General Kelly said was a lie."

There have been calls for General Kelly to apologize, but he has not, and the White House still contends that he won't. During those moments at the podium when he railed against the congresswoman's appearances on news shows concerning the president's remarks to Sgt. La David Johnson's family, General Kelly never used Congresswoman Wilson's name or official title. Congresswoman Wilson said, "He just kept referring to me as *she*."

There's been a noticeable, unavoidable, and conspicuous change in the dealings with Black America from the highest office in the land since 12:01 p.m., January 20, 2017. I think back to March 22, 2017. Reporters were asking the Congressional Black Caucus questions about their meeting with the president. The second-to-last question was from someone other than me, a White reporter in fact, asking Congressman Cedric Richmond, "Mr. Trump being accused of being a racist, encouraging White supremacists, coming out of this meeting, do you believe those things to be true?"

Congressman Richmond responded, saying, "You have to talk to the people who made those allegations, and ask them what they would say about it. I would tell you that he is the 45th president of the United States, and we talked about issues that were critically important to the African American community. We talked about divisive rhetoric that hurts the African Americans and that may cause more of a divide in this country."

But since that meeting, a multiplicity of issues and events have changed that dynamic. One major event (which I discussed earlier in these pages) for the history books came in early August 2017, in Charlottesville, Virginia. White supremacists, believers in White racial purity, clashed with people of good will and good intent. The target of those filled with hate was Black and Jewish America. These groups countered White racist rage over the removal of a statue of Robert E. Lee. The protest over the removal of this statue was a series of hate-filled marches of Nazis, Klansmen, and other White supremacists. This White rage left a woman murdered, a young White woman who believed in this country moving forward with all people together, not divided.

The atmosphere in Charlottesville, a beautiful quaint village I had visited a year earlier, in 2016, was now polluted. A jewelry shop owner I had become friends with had to take her sign down because it bears her name, a beautiful Jewish name. She is fearful of reprisal on her store if the White supremacists come back. Her shop is fifty yards from where the murder happened.

The president got it wrong as he spoke without his teleprompter script. He tried to clean it up at least six times, and it never worked because his heart was not in the spirit of unity. What stuck after all the speeches was the president saying, "There are some very fine people on both sides." Since when is a White supremacist or a member of the KKK or a Nazi a fine person? Well, if your dad was hooked up with these groups, as the president's father was, I guess that's what you would think. And David Duke, a former Grand Wizard of the KKK, supported the president's statement.

The president's indecision on Charlottesville affected his administration. Kenneth Frazier, the CEO of Merck, who happens to be Black, stepped down from the American Manufacturing Council in direct protest to the president's response to Charlottesville. President Trump, in turn, blasted on social media Mr. Frazier and the company he heads. Because of his business acumen, Kenneth Frazier has advised presidents of both parties. But at the end of the day, he was a Black man offended by Trump's lack of condemnation and his disgraceful, veiled support of a vile group of people that targeted others because they were not White.

Months later the issue of the Confederacy appeared again, this time with the president's chief of staff, John Kelly. General Kelly spoke of Robert E. Lee in glowing terms as a hero, when Lee had actually deserted the U.S. military to fight for his home state to keep slavery alive. Kelly also said that a compromise could have prevented the Civil War. First, any compromise would have kept slavery alive in the South. Second, the South fired first, on Fort Sumter, and that is where the war began.

The White House stood by Kelly's comment and challenged anyone to question the general. At this point, the question was begged: "Did this White House and the president believe slavery was wrong?" I asked that question as there was so much confusion on where the administration stood on this historic travesty. Slavery was, is, and will always be wrong and a grievous scar on any society that condones and participates in it. The current White House's record is spotty on history and equality. I asked that question on October 31, 2017, because Sarah Huckabee Sanders, the White House press secretary, left more questions than answers in that White House daily briefing when she made comments such as "Look, all of our leaders have flaws."

That and other comments seemed casual and flip, not acknowledging the weight of the haunts of the terror of slavery. The next day, I went at it again, this time getting her attention in a question-and-answer session. This was not like the day before when she ignored my hand and I asked the question as she was walking out the door. November 1, 2017, I asked, "Compromise. The issue of compromise. What's the definition of compromise as it relates to slavery and the Civil War?"

Huckabee Sanders offered, "Look, I'm not going to get in and relitigate the Civil War like I told you yesterday. I think I've addressed the concerns that a lot of people had and the questions that you had. I'm not going to relitigate history here."

I came back with:

> I'm asking a question, Sarah, seriously. The question is, "Does this administration believe, does the president believe slavery was wrong?" And before you answer, Mary Frances Berry, a historian, said in 1860 there was a compromise. The compromise was to have Southern states keep slavery, but the Confederacy fired on Fort Sumter that caused the Civil War. And because of the Civil War, what happened? The North won.

Huckabee Sanders ended the back and forth by saying, "I think it is disgusting and absurd to suggest that anyone inside of this building would support slavery."

Black issues swirled in 2017, like the accidental tourist at the White House who took center stage. The issue of "taking a knee" makes my blood boil because of how the president stole the narrative from Colin Kaepernick of how and why he knelt during the playing of the National Anthem at NFL games. The president said it was disrespectful to the soldiers, the anthem, and the flag. Well, Kaepernick did it to bring attention to the centuries-old problem of the community and police. Taking a knee was meant to bring attention to police-involved shootings of Blacks, which continues in 2018. An irony is that the Kerner Commission report on police violence is fifty years old this year, and Colin Kaepernick is taking a knee fifty years later. Nothing has changed.

The president of the United States, among his many duties and titles, is also considered a moral leader. Many say his morality on issues of Black America is bankrupt, particularly as he was accused of repeatedly offering a racist comment in a meeting of Democratic and Republican leaders.

The week of January 11, 2018, the president convened a meeting on the issue of DACA, the Deferred Action for Childhood Arrivals. This issue involves children who were brought to this country without proper documentation. About twenty-four leading members of both parties were assembled in the Cabinet Room in the White House. The president said he was working on what he called "a bill of love." This made some in his party upset about this being a possible pathway to citizenship

Later that week, Trump flipped the script in the discussion that was supposedly begun in good faith. The shift came when leaks started oozing out of a second meeting like pus from a horrible infection. The president was accused of repeatedly saying that he did not want people from "shithole countries" like Haiti, El Salvador, and all of Africa coming to America. However, he clearly stated that he wanted people from Norway. It was the White Meat versus Dark Meat discussion—not over poultry, but people. The White House and its apologists later tried to spin the discussion, saying the president's words were actually about a merit-based system. Really? The Center for American Progress has demonstrated that at least since 2012 Black immigrants have shown better education progress than any other immigrant groups. They have attained more degrees than even American citizens by birth. The White House point was moot.

I think back to Dr. Martin Luther King Jr. and his ultimate sacrifice for everyone, for first-class citizenship for Black people, including me, that has never been achieved. I think about Dr. King and Robert Kennedy, men of different races, cultures, and socioeconomic status. They were on the same path, and they were assassinated six weeks apart fifty years ago. These men, had they lived, planned to combine their efforts to attack poverty, beyond race and gender. Their insight is sorely needed as some of our politicians see this issue as a priority yet they still can't figure out the formula to lift people out of social and financial despair. How ironic that 2018 is also the fiftieth anniversary of the Poor People's Campaign.

On that day, January 12, to honor Dr. King and given the president's previous comments about "shithole countries," I had to ask the president if he was racist. And when I look back on it, it is a sad day to ever ask a sitting American president if he is a racist—but it was the perfect day to ask it. Dr. King used the idea of making people uncomfortable to move the plight of others to the forefront. This is what Colin Kaepernick had tried to do. It was "inconvenient" that day, but the truth of the question prevailed. The president didn't answer any of my four questions that day, nor did he answer the question from the other reporter about his "shithole" statement.

I was the only one who asked the president if he was a racist, and he walked out of the room as if he didn't hear me. But my press colleagues let me know he heard me, and the microphones heard me clearly. My words were so clear that people I'd never met but who hear my voice on radio and TV daily knew it was me. The president heard me! His answer came days later, after my question. And his lack of a response dominated the news cycles on the big shows of the major networks for days. The president's eventual answer was just like the one he gave to CNN's Don Lemon when he was a candidate for president: "I am not a racist. I am the least racist person."

But people weren't buying it. On January 18, 2018, the Congressional Black Caucus and Democrats from the House Judiciary Committee introduced a resolution to censure President Trump for what the resolution termed his racist "shithole" comments. The resolution had nearly 150 co-sponsors. Although censure does not offer legal consequences, it does give a public reprimand! That's something no one wants, particularly Trump, who prides himself on his image and brand.

Congressional Black Caucus head Cedric Richmond said, "Congress must speak with one voice in condemning these offensive and anti-American remarks. There is no excuse for it."

On March 22, 2017, Congressman Richmond didn't give an answer to the question if Trump was racist. However, today the answer by a leading Congressional Black Caucus member, civil rights icon John Lewis, is "Yes, President Trump is a racist." The answer by the NAACP is also that "President Trump is a racist," and the list goes on. The NAACP, the nation's oldest civil rights organization, defines racism as "the intersection of racial prejudice and power." They have officially assigned this most serious word to the president of the United States.

As for the Black agenda, where does it fit in with a president now termed as a racist? Moving forward, White House officials allege that 2018 will offer things like plans on school choice, economics to further cut into the Black unemployment rate, and work to cut the Black recidivism rate, which supposedly will be an effort to stop the cycle of a large portion of Black people entering and then reentering the criminal justice system.

Do I think the president can in earnestness and good faith overcome his missteps in 2017 with the Black community? I'm not sure. But he must begin by showing contrition. Then he must make significant, concrete efforts to change the perception that he alone has put in front of us as how we view him in Black America. It all boils down to action for the Black community, doing something to overcome and reverse the hundreds of years of racism.

Is the president a racist? If we look at his track record and use the definition from the NAACP, yes, he is. If I had to grade the president now, as I have done with presidents I've worked with in the past on their record on race, President Trump would get an F! But I believe in redemption. We saw a historic shift with Governor George Wallace as he lay on his deathbed. I just hope it won't take that long for this president.

Mr. President, you have time to make drastic changes. The Black community is a forgiving community, but at the same time we don't forget. We are waiting. What will you do?

· 7 ·

Education for All?

𝒯here needs to be a universal education on the subject of Historically Black Colleges and Universities (HBCUs). This fact was proven in 2017 during the outpouring of words and emotion from all sides of the spectrum in the build-up to the HBCU presidents' February meeting with President Donald Trump and that infamous Oval Office photo op. Confusion was laced with ire for those in support of HBCUs wanting tangible help and concern that the Trump administration would merely offer only lip service and use the meeting and photo op as a public relations opportunity. Those who were against the HBCUs felt there was too much attention paid to those schools instead of other issues. And some thought the HBCU system was racist because they simply didn't understand the need for HBCUs' existence. According to noted HBCU historian Marybeth Gasman, a professor at the University of Pennsylvania, HBCUs were created for a very obvious and much needed reason: "White institutions would not let Black people attend them."

As always, this was one of those stories I covered and simultaneously knew all too well as an alumna of an HBCU. I understood the HBCU mission before I stepped foot on campus as a student. I grew up on one of those college campuses that ultimately loved me to success. In the summer of 2017, I was recognized at my alma mater along with former Vice President Joe Biden with an honorary doctorate degree. I received a Doctor of Laws degree.

Jokes have a bit of truth in them, and this joke screams truth more than laughter. In the Black community, there is a hierarchy of thought: first there is God/Jesus, second are the HBCUs, and then there is Barack Obama. These three are lightning rods or third rails for anyone outside of the Black community who dares to touch or cross them in unkind ways. From its inception, the Trump administration has thrown darts at at least two in this triad: Barack Obama and HBCUs. (When it comes to throwing darts at God/Jesus, Trump is not much of a church-goer.)

Many in the Black community have become unofficial curators and overseers of HBCUs because these universities have been the major source of catapulting Blacks into the middle class in this country. Much care has been taken to preserve and further the legacy built by people wanting to educate the future generations of slaves. Such was the case in some states like North Carolina from 1830 to 1831. Its General Assembly passed laws to prevent slaves from being educated. There was punishment for slaves and slaveholders for slave literacy in states like Virginia, Mississippi, and South Carolina. Despite these laws, some slaves slipped through the cracks and learned to read and write. One HBCU president, Glenda Glover of Tennessee State University, says some of the early schools started in churches, homes, and rundown schoolhouses using the few resources they had. However, some slaveholders desired slave literacy for religious instruction because they viewed Christian teachings and Bible reading as their duty. Therefore, some of the earliest HBCUs were founded as religious schools and then became institutions that educated a large portion of Blacks in this nation.

The passion for HBCUs is rooted in the connections to slavery as we are the hopes and dreams of those Africans who were held in bondage in this country hundreds of years ago. Any attempts, consciously or unconsciously, to thwart the education of Blacks in this county is met with a fierce fight because of the history stemming from the deadly inhumanity of slavery. During slavery, the first HBCUs were founded in the North, in Pennsylvania, with Cheney University founded in 1852 by Quakers and Lincoln University in 1854. Lincoln University's website states that it is the first degree-issuing HBCU in the nation. Then there is Wilberforce University in Ohio, established in 1856, the first college to be owned and operated by Blacks and by the Methodist Episcopal Church and the African Methodist Episcopal Church. Marybeth Gasman says that Wilberforce is also the "first Black college" to have a Black president at the helm.

In 1865, approximately two years after President Lincoln signed the Emancipation Proclamation, nine more HBCUs were founded:

Alabama State University, Barber-Scotia College, Fayetteville State University, Howard University, Johnson C. Smith University, Morehouse, Morgan State University, St. Augustine's University, and Talladega College. In 2017, those nine HBCUs celebrated 150 years of existence.

The secret of freedom for slaves through the Emancipation Proclamation had been kept from them for two years, extending the tyranny and unjust profit for slave owners while slaves did not know they had been released from forced, unpaid servitude. But where would they go when freedom was a reality? The spirit of the slave yearned for more, with a desire to rise higher and beyond their deplorable conditions. At that time, however, there were few avenues, if any, for slaves in the South to live a life of first-class citizenship.

While looking through each school's history and learning how the schools were established, I found that some of the schools were organized to educate ministers or have links to religion. These include Morgan State University, Barber-Scotia College, Johnson C. Smith University, and Alabama State University. Some of the other schools were harder to form because the founders or financial contributors were Black and/or former slaves. At least one former slave was a founder of Morehouse. Talladega had two former slaves involved with its founding. Blacks were also involved in the founding of Alabama State University and Fayetteville State University.

Howard University was founded as a federal land grant school set up for the education of the descendants of slaves. The Morrill Act, which offered land grants, passed in July 1862. Through the Morrill Act, seventeen HBCUs were established. The act made it possible for new Western states to establish colleges for their citizens. The new land grant institutions, which emphasized agriculture and mechanic arts, opened opportunities to thousands of farmers and working people previously excluded from higher education.

When it came to the founding of my alma mater, Morgan State University, I learned the following. Before the seating of the initial meeting of the nine all-White Board of Trustees of the Centenary Biblical Institute, five Black pastors emerged with the vision for establishing the Bible college that began classes with nine African American men. The five who began the process to establish the Bible college were the Rev. Benjamin Brown, Rev. Samuel Green Sr., Rev. Elijah Grissem,

Rev. James Harper, and Rev. James Peck. This Bible college eventually became Morgan State University.

Morgan State University also cites more in-depth information on the injustices done to one of the founders, Rev. Samuel Green Sr., who yearned for something considered so simple today, to read a book. Green purchased his freedom in 1833. He was a conductor on the Underground Railroad. He assisted his son Samuel Green Jr. in escaping from slavery to Canada in 1854. In 1857, Rev. Green Sr. was arrested and incarcerated for possessing a copy of the controversial anti-slavery novel *Uncle Tom's Cabin*, by Harriet Beecher Stowe.

According to Dr. Edwin Johnson of the Maryland Commission on African American History and Culture, St. Mary's College in Maryland is finding its links to slavery and its officials had to rethink how they would construct the school's newly anticipated stadium because remnants of slaves had been found on the site. The findings were those of daily life, a cup and other artifacts from that time. The school that was once a female seminary owned slaves.

On the flip side, as Blacks took the pain of slavery and were not allowed by law to read and write, their blood, sweat, tears, and torture-filled lives worked toward educating the masses, White America, with prestigious schools.

In March 2016, Harvard University retired one of its symbols, a shield modeled on the family crest of Isaac Royall Jr., an eighteenth-century slaveholder whose bequest endowed the first professorship of law at Harvard. Research on Royall gives news that he owned a lucrative sugar plantation on the West Indian Island of Antigua. That plantation was worked by African slaves.

On April 18, 2017, Georgetown University apologized for its role in the 1838 sale of 272 enslaved individuals for the university's financial gain. The atonement took place in the presence of more than one hundred descendants of those enslaved individuals. Georgetown University has taken several corrective actions hundreds of years later to include renaming an existing building Isaac Hawkins Hall after the first enslaved person listed in the 1838 sale document.

To further drive home the point, a September 27, 2013, NPR report titled "How Slavery Shaped America's Oldest and Most Elite Colleges" asserts that Brown University was named after a merchant family. It is reported they were not a huge slave trade family but were connected to profiting from it, as were many more of the elite schools in this nation like Harvard, Princeton, Columbia, Yale, Dartmouth, University of Pennsylvania, and William and Mary. The story also offered that the essence and foundation of the racism that slavery was or played on was the perceived inferiority of one race over another.

Fast forward to the claims made by Betsy DeVos, Trump's education secretary, in February 2017, the first months of the Trump administration. She said Blacks were the "real pioneers" in school choice. Understanding our history shows we had no choice in education, but we overcame anyway.

Marybeth Gasman has been studying HBCUs for twenty-four years. She contends that the lack of understanding about the history of HBCUs is about being complacent versus embracing the truth of the correlation between slavery, literacy, and the historic Black schools. Gasman declares, "I think often times people just conveniently forget [the history] because it makes them feel a little bit better."

On the other hand, she says some people lack the knowledge; "a lot of people just don't understand how HBCUs began." She says, "We needed Black institutions because White institutions would not let Black people attend them." She goes on to explain: "Public Black colleges were set up as systems of segregation because Blacks were not legally allowed into White institutions and they were discriminated against during Jim Crow and segregation because of vile racism in our country. And then the private ones were set up because Blacks were not allowed into private White institutions either. After slavery you had this huge population of African Americans who were denied formal education and so you have Black colleges that were set up by a whole variety of entities to educate Blacks."

HBCUs were born, and supporters of the schools worked for them to thrive. The mission was not to divide but to bridge the divides. Gasman's extensive research has found "most people consider HBCUs to be segregated environments." But she points out that some of the schools had "never ever been segregated, except when they were forced to by southern law. So, there were some southern states that couldn't have Whites or other non-Blacks going to HBCUs. And so that was the only time. Other than that, HBCUs have never been segregated . . . I think what has happened—When people think of segregation, of the fall of segregation with *Brown vs. Board* or at least the legal fall of segregation, right, they often think that, *Oh! That means we don't have any more organizations that are all Black.* They think of segregation as being all Black. They don't think of segregation as necessarily these White institutions that were keeping people out a lot of times. For example, there are lots and lots of colleges and universities across the country that have very few African Americans in their college enrollment or other people of color, and yet we don't think of them as segregated institutions."

But with Black schools, it is just the reverse. They are considered racist and supporters of segregation. The following comments by Marybeth Gasman speak to this point: "While many people think of Black colleges as segregated institutions even though they are 13 percent White and 2 percent Asian and 3 percent Latino and then you've got an international population and you also have great diversity in terms of the Black population: Caribbean and African and African American and people from Brazil. There's lots and lots of diversity there in terms of religious and sexuality, etc."

Before Marybeth Gasman made that statement, the late Supreme Court justice Antonin Scalia offered in an opinion that Blacks need to stay at HBCUs because they do better there. I had to listen to the audio of Scalia's comments from a December 11, 2015, story by CNN Politics titled "Supreme Court Releases Audio of Justice Antonin Scalia Saying Maybe Black Students Don't Belong at Elite Universities." Scalia said African Americans might be better off instead at "less advanced or a slower track school where they do well." The late justice even remarked in a brief that "most of the Black scientists in this country don't come from schools like the University of Texas, but from lesser schools where they do not feel that they're being pushed ahead in classes that are too fast for them." He went on to say, "I don't think it stands to reason that it's a good thing for the University of Texas to admit as many Blacks as possible. I just don't."

After Scalia's statement, the audio provided another justice's verbal public rejection of Scalia's words. Justice Scalia had a warped version of the facts. Gasman says yes, HBCUs have produced more Black doctors, scientists, teachers, and nurses. However, as Gasman says of the controversial comments by Scalia, "African Americans are earning degrees at all types of institutions across the country in science. The problem is at many institutions they are not being treated equally, number one. They are experiencing a lot of micro aggressions on a daily basis. They are not respected by many faculty and their peers and there is evidence of this. So, one of the things that happens is that, yeah, HBCUs do a much better job of African Americans in sciences. It doesn't have to do with being slow. It has to do with the institution taking responsibility for the education of their students and realizing all the responsibility does not fall on the student, but a lot of the responsibility for learning falls on the institution."

When people in high positions get the facts wrong on HBCUs, it is damning for the educational system. If those who make policy and laws don't understand, then the system cannot flourish. The reason why the schools continued to grow was due to Jim Crow and segregation in the South that supported the separation of races in education. This leads to the next point.

There is such irony in how Ivy League schools thrive and still profit off the foundations of slavery while HBCUs struggle to remain open, with descendants of slaves looking to education as a partial promise of the future. Dr. Glenda Glover, president of Tennessee State University, an HBCU, contends in 2018, "Some HBCUs are drowning in debt and financial need." She was one of the HBCU presidents curious about what the White House would offer financially to help HBCUs in that 2017 meeting with the president and White House officials.

This as the number of HBCUs has dwindled from 122 to 105 because of a hard, monetary hit. Currently, North Carolina A&T is the largest HBCU in the nation. The prayer is for help to sustain these educational and social touchstones. When the calls and invitations came for the HBCU presidents to meet with President Trump at the end of February 2017, the schools questioned if it was real, understanding what was at stake. Several schools were floundering, wondering if they would close at the time of the meeting.

HBCUs and their funding has been a major issue since their inception. Looking back at the Obama presidency, early in that administration, bills providing funding to HBCUs were allowed to sunset. Later in the Obama administration, a worker at the Department of Education (DoE) found a loophole in Parent PLUS, a student loan program, that caused DoE to revamp the program. This resulted in the schools losing millions of dollars and students because credit for school loans to families was denied if they had any blemishes, even the smallest discrepancy, on their credit report.

Cedric Richmond, head of the Congressional Black Caucus, speaking of those in the DoE at the time, says, "Most of them just don't understand the value they [HBCUs] bring to the kids and how they change lives, and it is not just that kid's life, it's a generation."

The Obama administration worked to try to correct the mistake. However, former Morgan State University president, Dr. Earl S. Richardson, says, "That was not enough, and it has never been enough" by way of federal funding for these schools.

Due to the inequity in funding for HBCUs, Dr. Richardson, who led Morgan State for twenty-six years, has been at the forefront of a lawsuit for parity in funding for Black schools as opposed to White schools. Richardson was the lead in the Coalition for Equity and Excellence in Maryland Higher Education against the Maryland Higher Education Commission. Coalition members include Morgan State, Bowie State University, Coppin State University, and the University of Maryland Eastern Shore. Regarding the HBCU equity lawsuit, Richardson is on record saying to the Morgan State University Alumni Association, "There's no question there's a great disparity in the amount of investments made by the state between the historically Black colleges and universities and the traditionally White institutions." He describes the difference as "woefully lacking." This disparity has cut into Black schools' chances at grants and private contracts and new and continuing students.

Richmond is convinced that his mother "would have gone bankrupt a million times if it would have meant for my brother and I to get a degree from Morehouse." He says the thinking was that a degree would change their lives forever for the better. By the way, Richmond is a 1995 graduate of Morehouse College.

During the presidential campaigning for 2016 at the Cleveland Convention, there was a list of events for reporters and supporters to participate in. One was an event for HBCUs. I attended the daytime session in a hot church with no air conditioning. The sanctuary was filled with those eager to hear about what could be. A Black neighborhood was the backdrop of this offering of future sustainable hope for Black institutions of higher learning. The conversation was about these 105 schools that propel a majority of Black people to middle-income status. After all was said and done, before the mostly Black attendants left to go back to the Cleveland Convention venue, the only commitment made was to keep HBCUs viable.

Fast forward to February 27, 2017. The effort by the Trump administration was to craft an executive order by the end of the month, Black History Month. The search was under way as staff looked through old executive orders and initiatives on HBCUs from prior administrations. They even examined what President Ronald Reagan had done by putting a spotlight on HBCUs and putting it directly in the purview of the vice president's office, according to Paris Dennard of the Thurgood Marshall Fund. During the time this was going on, Dennard was a wealth of insight, as he was during the Republican convention.

The White House wanted buy-in with this. They wanted validation from the HBCUs on their efforts to help HBCUs financially. The White House wanted to welcome them to a meeting. It was initially said the president would meet with them. However, the red flags started flying. The HBCU presidents were concerned about the meeting, not wanting just a photo op but to leave with something of substance. Many of the HBCU presidents were wary of the meeting. Well, the meeting happened. The sixty or so HBCU presidents came to the White House. They met with then–presidential advisor Steve Bannon, who pledged that Trump officials wanted to help. He told the HBCU presidents to give the administration a list of wants and it would make it happen. Tennessee State University president Glenda Glover was part of the group and remembers Reince Priebus in the room for the session. Glover says, "The administration folks said it was about building a bridge. 'We are going to work diligently with you to ensure that there is a relationship between the HBCUs and the White House.'"

The list of HBCU wants had been compiled by the HBCU presidents and were given to the Thurgood Marshall Fund, at the time led by Johnnie Taylor. Taylor, in turn, gave the written list to the White House. In the meeting, Glover says she personally asked the White House "to establish a fund of $25 billion for HBCUs. It would include several things. One would be to provide an incentive for students to remain in the STEM field—science, technology, engineering, and math—if they maintain a cumulative GPA of 3.0 or above in that first two years of college, then they would go to the university for the next two years at no cost." There was also a request for "year-round Pell

Grants and Title III funding." A Pell Grant is a federal program that provides money for lower-income students to attend college. (Months later, without the help of the White House, Congress did pass a request from the presidents to make funding for Pell Grants year-round to include the summer sessions.)

Meanwhile, on May 19, 2015, a *Washington Post* article, "Minorities and Poor College Students Are Shouldering the Most Student Debt," cited a study called "The Debt Divide: The Racial and Class Bias Behind the 'New Normal' of Student Borrowing" that reported "eighty-four percent of college students with Pell Grants graduate from four-year public schools with debt, compared with less than half of students without the need-based grants." Getting into the racial aspect, "less than two-thirds of White graduates from public schools borrow; four out of five Black graduates take out loans for college. And Black students who do borrow come out with more debt than their peers."

Also, according to a report in the *Journal of Blacks in Higher Education*, "Pell Grants: The Cornerstone of African-American Higher Education": "In 2008 more than 155,000 students at the nation's Historically Black Colleges and Universities received federal Pell Grants for low-income students. In fact, at a majority of all-Black colleges, two-thirds or more of all enrolled students receive federal Pell Grants." Student funding is a big help in retention, to keep the kids in school with the ultimate goal of graduation.

These institutions also need increased funding for infrastructure because many of the campuses are old and outdated. There is also a search for funding for the HBCU research institutions to keep the mission going and to be competitive with other research schools.

Glover offers an understanding into the requests, saying, "Title Three deals with student success, to make sure you have enough funding available for minority students to be successful through college. We wanted to ensure that they made enough funding available. Most of the HBCUs are participants in the Title Three program." The HBCU presidents wanted to leave the White House "no worse off" than when they came for that highly publicized session, according to Glover.

But later there was a gathering in the Oval Office with the president for pictures. The Thurgood Marshall Fund and the White House point person on HBCUs had been working to make it happen. The HBCU presidents were herded around the office like cattle, with the president reportedly wanting the female presidents close to him, behind the desk. The educational leaders were eventually arranged around the Resolute desk, the desk that a toddler John Kennedy Jr. had been photographed crawling under so long ago. The picture was taken of a grinning President Trump and the HBCU presidents. For some of the educators, the photo was a dagger in the back, as their alumni, community, and supporters chastised them for going and succumbing to a photo op and not coming back with money for some of the floundering schools.

So many people criticized the meeting—especially after that photo of Kellyanne Conway perched on the sofa in the Oval Office during that historic meeting, her shoes off and knees spread apart. Later, the White House organizers working with the HBCU initiative said they had never promised money and they would have to wait for Congress to act. But the White House had made the HBCU presidents believe they would be getting money. So as the can was being kicked down the road, the next step was to wait for the executive order and hope for funding. There was a lot of anticipation, but early that month I learned there was no money in that order.

When the executive order was issued at the end of February, there were no carve-outs of money for the schools. It was so bad that the schools had considered not working with the organizations that corralled them for the meeting, organizations like the National Association for Equal Opportunity in Higher Education (NAFEO), which itself was in need of $2 million for its building, and the Thurgood Marshall Fund, which received $26.5 million from the Koch brothers that was not ear-marked primarily for the HBCUs. The money, a five-year allotment, was for the creation of a Center for Advancing Opportunity, which would focus on education, criminal justice, entrepreneurship, and other issues affecting what it called fragile communities. The United Negro College Fund (UNCF) was the bastard child of that trio; the stronger connection was between the White House and NAFEO and the Thurgood Marshall Fund. The UNCF, the older of the HBCU advocate groups, was left out of much of the conversation with the other advocate groups and the White House. Those who benefitted from anything to come from it were first, the Thurgood Marshall Fund, and then NAFEO, if at all because of its alliance with the person who brought it all together, Omarosa Mani-gault. This debacle likely added to the reason she was eventually fired (or forced to resign) in December of that same year.

Immediately following the release of the order, Morgan State University president David Wilson issued a statement saying, "After reading the Executive Order, there is nothing in it that is substantively different than what has been in other HBCU Executive Orders. I was expecting More! And no, I was not at the White House today when the order was signed as some of you have been asking me."

There were lots of statements that day revolving around the disappointment of no money that people were led to believe would be coming. Congressman Elijah Cummings, a Howard University graduate who also sits on the board of regents for Morgan State University, offered in a statement, "HBCUs need more than empty rhetoric and photo ops." The Root.com from March 2, 2015, had a story in which the then–president of Morehouse College was quoted as saying, "We got played!"

Needless to say, people were so upset. It was beyond bad. Understanding the history and the current, very real financial struggles of the schools that are educating roughly 370,000 students in 2017, the schools were looking for a significant financial infusion.

Now that we know the facts about Historically Black Colleges and Universities, their mission of the past, and the direct link to slavery, the current question is: Are HBCUs still needed? Marybeth Gasman says, "We absolutely need HBCUs today." Gasman explains that "HBCUs in many ways are offering an environment that is empowering during a very difficult time where Black people are being assaulted by police and blamed for society's problems, etc."

Also, there needs to be vigilance for current forms of segregation that may not mirror the past but are just as real. Dr. Edwin Johnson of the Maryland Commission on African American History and Culture says that one racial divider is the Scholastic Aptitude Test (SAT) scores, and Gasman offers another nuance to Dr. Johnson's statements, saying it is also classist as many of the schools that are not SAT-optional weed out people with those scores. Studies show that Black and Brown students and those in the underserved communities do not fare as well on these standardized tests for college entrance.

With the understanding of the past and the present, what will be the future of these treasured and essential schools? In this administration, their future hangs in the balance.

· 8 ·

Divided Nation

*T*here are certain images, words, phrases, fragrances, songs, movies, and events that help us recall different moments in our lives. We remember when Neil Armstrong and Buzz Aldrin left their footprints on the moon. We remember where we were and maybe what it smelled like when we got the grim news that President John F. Kennedy, Dr. Martin Luther King Jr., Bobby Kennedy, and Malcolm X were killed. We remember seeing and hearing when Barack Obama was elected the 44th president of the United States. We also remember when Donald Trump was elected as the 45th president of this nation. We had no idea of the changes to come. We've had to brace ourselves for upheaval domestically and internationally, especially in areas like foreign policy and immigration, which often seems like a way to racially target Black and Brown people.

The last period of rapid racial progress in this nation was the civil rights movement, fifty years ago. Most importantly, since then people of all races have worked together for inclusion and to end barriers. Now, President Trump has begun to take us backward, erecting barriers. In 1987, Republican president Ronald Reagan declared to Russian president Mikhail Gorbachev, "Mr. Gorbachev, tear down this wall!" Back then, it was about peace and freedom. Any new expensive wall erected by this president on our southern border will be the polar opposite of what President Reagan was trying to create: unity and inclusiveness.

P. J. Crowley, an assistant secretary of state under Hillary Clinton, author of *Red Line: American Foreign Policy in a Time of Fractured Politics and Failing States*, proffers:

The challenge today is that we have taken an already complex and divisive issue and invested it with a host of national concerns, both real and imagined. Candidate Donald Trump was able to pull many of these policy threads together in a way that appealed to a diverse but critical mass of voters. He channeled public concerns about lost jobs, declining wages, terrorism, international crime, the opioid epidemic, unfair trade, and taxes under the rubric of national sovereignty and border security. His proposed solution involved reinforcement of borders in a globalized world that had made borders too porous. His bill of particulars included the wall, the ban, better trade deals, and the repatriation of tax revenue and jobs. Trump is hardly the first president to promise a crackdown on illegal immigration. But he has tried to erase the political distinction between illegal and legal immigration, the former in the interest of law and order and the latter in the interest of national security. Of course, reality is very different than the one Trump portrays. He dismisses the socio-economic importance of immigration, keeping our working population younger as the baby boomers retire. And he ignores the push and pull behind global migration. The push relates to the disintegration of fragile countries due to conflict and climate change. The pull involves the unmet need for low skill work within the United States at a time of effective full employment, which existing immigration quotas can't meet due to political paralysis. Given the political polarization, the parties talk past one another. Calls for comprehensive immigration reform are blunted by accusations of amnesty. Thus, there is no reasoned debate and little room for compromise.

So, what happens when immigrants are deported and the jobs they hold are unfilled? Will employers pay higher wages for "American" workers, or will the companies have problems because they can't afford the wage hike? These are questions that have yet to be answered because the situation is on the precipice and the future is not yet seen. Beyond the socioeconomics of it all, and this "America First" idea of Trump's, the racism is real. The fight over the president's immigration efforts to send anyone undocumented "back where they came from," especially the Dreamers, children who do not know their homeland, feels ugly, bitter, and racial!

The evidence for Trump's racism has been easy to detect. On January 30, 2018, in his State of the Union Address, the president said this from the Well of the House of Representatives: "There are Americans that are dreamers too." There was a need for concern: That same night

David Duke, the former Grand Wizard of the Ku Klux Klan (KKK), tweeted this response: "Thank you President Trump. Americans are Dreamers too."

Former Republican National Committee chair Michael Steele affirmed in an interview for American Urban Radio Networks months earlier that this White House wants to "control the browning of America." If you believe that is extreme, here's a fact to chew on. We are a nation now seeing the majority of children born in this country as "minority" babies. The Pew Research Center predicts that the combined minority groups (Hispanics, Asians, African Americans) will collectively be a majority by the year 2055. The U.S. Census Bureau puts that even earlier, in 2044. That's a scary proposition for a group that has been the majority for centuries, and people are afraid.

Another part of the current debate on immigration is over the "visa lottery" of people from countries like those in Africa, and parts of Asia versus European countries, which have traditionally sent fewer immigrants. P. J. Crowley writes, "At one level, notwithstanding America's narrative as a nation of immigrants, this tension has always been present, often below the surface but periodically raising its ugly head above the surface. We do assimilate foreign born people as Americans quite effectively. It is a national strength. But there has always been resistance. Across all ethnicities and creeds, some sub-section of the population has felt threatened by the latest wave of immigration. Race and culture are part of it. So too are economic opportunity, political power and self-identity."

People forget we're a nation made up of natives, immigrants, and slaves. Everyone didn't see Lady Liberty when they came here. What I find so hard to believe is that people who aren't indigenous to this land want to kick other people out. I am a Black woman, five generations removed from the last known slave in my family, Joseph Dollar Brown, from my mother's side. I therefore find this asinine and personally insulting!

Donald Trump's percolating racist attitudes toward immigrants also play into issues of national security. The president held conversations with both Democrats and Republicans in front of the cameras, on January 11, 2018. People were mesmerized by what looked like transparency. But days later, with no cameras or audio equipment around, there was another story. This was a story of "shithole" countries: Norway versus El Salvador, Haiti, and Africa.

I remember once going into an upscale, family-owned store. The owner, a person who was clearly upset, started off the conversation expressing great concern for the inner city. But then she used that to segue into, "Why can't we take care of our own?" She began crying over this America First idea without mentioning the president. I was shocked as she was clearly someone whose family had migrated to the United States. I listened as she cried. I listened and listened, and then I asked her, "What are you doing to help fix these issues?"

She said, "Well, we hire people, and we do some things."

I listened for about fifteen minutes to her tearful argument. Then I said, "Do you realize if we push folks away, what happens when there's a major issue like 9/11 in this nation? Will they come? Will they help?" I also told her that too many people from the national intelligence community have said, "It is a matter of when and not if another attack will happen here."

There's a strong national security component to all this. Yes, we say "America First!" We must assume the responsibility for our own! But how are we hurting ourselves when we do that? If we push people out of our nation or prevent them from coming, if we call their citizens names and disparage their country because they are people who don't look like some of us, then we're entering hazardous territory. The debate on immigration must be had. The America First pledge by this president is emblazoned everywhere. Now the delicate dance ensues with relationships globally. Listening to those national intelligence sources, that dance could ultimately isolate us at our time of greatest need.

Our current situation is a delicate one. The United States used to be viewed as the "mature one" at the negotiation table. Now we're viewed as the petulant child. Our once strong European allies are viewing us with that questioning side-eye of disbelief. Mature and civil conversations need to be had on the matter of immigration. When we debate the issue of the visa lottery versus a merit-based pathway to citizenship, the facts must be on the table. What we don't need are racist feelings when there's talk of keeping people from other countries, especially Muslim countries, from coming to the United States.

Here's a stunning yet documented fact that is grossly under-reported. The Center for American Progress published an article on January 12, 2018, titled "The Top 3 Things You Need to Know about Black Immigrants in the United States in 2018." The report used data from a 2016 American Community Survey. The findings were that the 3.7 million Black immigrants in the United States have high rates of education and employment. The report shows that Black immigrants are more likely than all other immigrants to have some college education, or at least an associate's degree (29 percent compared with 19 percent). The education attainment rates for Black immigrants are like those for native-born Americans at 32 percent and 31 percent, respectively. Black immigrants are more likely to be active in the labor force than all other groups of immigrants: almost three-quarters (73 percent) of Black immigrants sixteen and older are in the labor force, compared with 67 percent of all immigrants and 64 percent of native-born Americans.

The report also said the Trump administration ended DACA on September 5, 2017. Overall, nearly eleven thousand DACA recipients are from countries where more than half of their immigrants to the United States are Black. Additionally, the Migration Policy Institute estimates that roughly 3 percent or thirty-six thousand African immigrants would have been eligible for DACA had they been registered. This means that the population of Black Dreamers, and thus of all people who would have been eligible for the Dream Act, is potentially much higher than those currently protected by DACA.

All of this dispels the notion that immigrant Blacks, and in fact all immigrants, are not contributing to society. These facts cut into the economic arguments the White House has used to support a merit-based system. But people, including some in the religious sector, contend that "We should only care for our own!"

Does the president care about these facts, or is he oblivious to them on matters of race? Who is there to help him in his ever-changing staff? One of the major issues for the Black community dealing with this White House is that there's no credible Black person they can go to in this administration. Former Republican Oklahoma congressman J. C. Watts, who is Black, says, "There is a lack of trust to start with." In other words, there's no one in the White House to communicate with the Black community in a way that the Black community will feel it's substantive and real. Watts continues, "And I think it has set back Black

Republicans, those of us who have worked hard over the last twenty years trying to build deeper relationships with the African American Community." He adds, "You don't have people in the White House like Kay Coles James and Michael Steele. There is a new breed of Black Republican."

What's so crazy is the kind of Black people who were out there supporting the president on immigration and race when the facts were apparent. One African American Republican in support of the Trump merit-based system is Paris Dennard, formerly of the George W. Bush administration. As of February 2018, his full-time job for several years has been with an organization, the Thurgood Marshall Fund, which lobbies for Historically Black Colleges and Universities (HBCUs)!

While all the controversy swirled around the president and his statements about the Black and Brown countries versus Norway, I found the discourse before the American public very interesting. The irony is that many of the HBCUs Paris Dennard is supposed to work for have a large contingent of international students. Their tuition is a large portion of the revenues of these schools. HBCU presidents were not happy at all about Dennard's conflict of interest and made their feelings known to the Thurgood Marshall Fund.

That entire "shithole" statement President Trump made, and which credible lawmakers said did occur, loomed large over the beginning of 2018. The remark overshadowed the entire immigration debate. There were real questions from both Democrats and Republicans. Could they work in good faith with a president who views this whole discussion on immigration from such a skewed vantage point?

The week of January 10, 2018, the Trump administration was building up to something unprecedented for them, transparency in the immigration process. They allowed the pool, a small contingent of the White House press corps, to stay in the room for about fifty-five minutes to hear the conversation over how to move immigration reform forward. There were portions of a meeting with Democratic and Republican leaders back and forth on camera. It was appreciated, as the American people want to be included in the process of debating policy that concerns the nation. People want to see and hear for themselves what is going on in the White House, particularly the goings-on in this embattled administration.

During the conversation, we saw a president who kept it together even as the sensational tell-all book *Fire and Fury* had recently been published saying that he was considered childish by senior staff and essentially was not mentally fit for the office. That first day, it was a real victory for the White House as it relates to the winning picture, the image of the president actually discussing a policy and not dictating it. There were conversations about DACA and Dreamers. During that week, the discussion was also about the southern border wall and how Mexico would still be made to pay for it through the NAFTA deal (which he has said in several of his events).

But then the veneer began to peel away, the structure started falling off bit by bit, and then by Thursday it was a crumpled heap. Apparently, President Trump could not sustain the image of a calm negotiator willing to be involved in policy give-and-take to come up with possible solutions. On January 11, when the cameras were not around, the immigration conversation went south, way south. Just eleven days into the new year, the president managed to offend those in the room with damning language, allegedly calling the continent of Africa, Haiti, and El Salvador shitholes or shithouses (whatever you believe). His point was that he did not want residents of those countries that he had labeled to be in this nation. Then in the same breath, he spoke glowingly about the people of Norway, a White majority country. It was White versus Black and Brown, and it was real, and it was scary. Political leaders in the meeting could not refrain from sharing what the president had allegedly said. Senator Dick Durbin and attorneys involved confirmed the president's remarks. Others in the meeting, all coincidentally of the Republican Party, could not seem to recall it being said originally, but few (if any) denied it.

President Trump is not new to wanting to keep people away when they do not look like him. This president worked to put in place a ban on people from Muslim nations coming to this country, and he did it in the name of trying to keep terrorism down. That's an old racist trick of trying to disguise the act by covering it up with a different issue—this time terrorism. Now he attributed his derogatory words about people from Black and Brown nations as a way to justify his radical immigration policy.

This Archie Bunker type of thinking was evident by too many influencers who were seeing and saying the same thing. The irony is that the point of the TV show *All in the Family* and the prejudice mentality of Archie Bunker was the joke of the show. He was the racist surrounded by reasonable people who tried to help him see the error of his ways, and it was played for laughs. In real life, it's not a laughing matter, especially when that person is the president of the country. In Donald Trump language, the shit hit the fan. The question was posed on the saddest of days.

It was the day the president recognized Dr. Martin Luther King Jr., January 12. President Trump held a signing ceremony recognizing the dreamer Dr. Martin Luther King Jr. A proclamation was made to make the King historic site a national park. The proclamation expanded the masonic temple as part of the park. The temple is the site of the first Southern Christian Leadership Conference offices. This is something the King family had wanted for years. Meanwhile, understanding who Dr. King was and how he had fought so hard for Black America, and all of America, I had to make a decision about the question I had been thinking about asking. This was one of the most significant King Day events that I have ever been a part of, and it meant a lot to me and many others.

In the 1980s, I was matriculating through Morgan State University, working toward my college degree. I was honored when I was asked to be one of the hosts of the MLK Day observance. Rosa Parks was in attendance, and Stevie Wonder gave the keynote speech and later sang some of his songs. Filmmaker and then–college classmate David Talbert was supposed to be my cohost, but he had an event in New Jersey that he could not turn down. So, I was the host all by myself. There are parts of that day that stick out in my mind. I remember some of the speakers, like then-Baltimore mayor Kurt Schmoke. And then-Bethel AME pastor John R. Bryant offered a message that has stuck with me for decades later. I use his words in some speeches that I am asked to give today. He called on all Dreamers and talked of those with "dis-ease," those with an unsettled future. Today those words resound clearly, more than thirty years later. Calling all Dreamers!

I was sure that I wanted to ask the question, but it had to be the right time and place. I likely wouldn't get an answer, I was aware of that, but on this day, as important as it is every year, I felt it was the right thing to do. I am one of the few minorities in that White House briefing room, so who else would do it? I decided to ask my question, "Are you a racist?" only after several issues had occurred. There had been a clear pattern of items that were race-based, culminating with the nation being in an uproar over the racially charged comments comparing Norway with Africa, Haiti, and El Salvador.

Most of us understand that migration to this nation is primarily about obtaining a better life, often after natural disasters or a way to better their circumstances with more opportunities so they can provide for their family. Demographer Roderick Harrison says people flee for their lives with immigration often a direct result of the ravages of war and famine. Those truly extreme and dire conditions drive people out of a given region in search for something better. He says that is the case for migration to the United States from places like Central America. As it relates to Haiti, it was the "the earthquake, other disasters, and the political oppression."

Harrison says that as we look at the issues of immigration, economics is front and center, playing a key role in the issue. There are poor economic opportunities that lead people to seek better situations. Clearly, that has been the major driver of immigration from Mexico and Central America to the United States in recent decades.

For example, he says that during the Great Recession, the Mexico economy "stabilized" while the United States struggled to try to fix the financial downturn. As a result, there was not an increase in immigration from that country to the United States as there had been during years of economic stability in the United States. He says, "People were better off staying there [Mexico] than coming here."

It is never advised to pit any group against another, but after the comments about Black and Brown countries versus the predominately White residents of Norway, something had to be said, but I didn't expect what I heard. Weeks later, General John Kelly, chief of staff, said that "undocumenteds" who have not registered themselves were "lazy asses." People in leadership positions and places, who we are accustomed to look to for maturity and clear thought, are engaging in stereotyping and negative, hurtful language with no facts to support it.

However, Harrison does offer a reasonable theory about low-income Americans and low-paying jobs that is similar to what was surprisingly said by Mexico's then-President Vicente Fox during the George W. Bush Administration. In 2005, Fox said Mexican immigrants take the jobs that not even Blacks want to do. People were up in arms over this politically charged and inaccurate statement, but Harrison offers support for what was said with the broader context that applied to all Americans, not just Black America. He says, "Unskilled immigrants are taking jobs, certainly in agriculture and food processing, and domestic work that Americans no longer want, even low-skilled Americans." So where are the opportunities for Americans of any race? Many of those jobs are off the radar for the poor. Many of them would have to relocate in order to take them.

"Immigrants are spending all the money they earn buying food, and clothing, things that support businesses and helps keep jobs running that eventually help people buy homes," he says. "Immigrants are supporting industries. Two thirds of the economy is consumer spending and in the United States, Europe and Japan, the native-born populations are shrinking there. The economy in fact needs more people to keep up consumer demand for products. So, without immigration, if Trump succeeded in slowing the rate of immigration, it might in fact reduce economic growth in the country."

What is happening now, those who are looking for opportunity for a better life coming from other countries now look to places like Canada for fear of deportation in the United States. No, it can't be a wide-open door, but isn't there a compromise? Isn't there a solution to determine how someone who works so hard to come to the United States can apply to stay, especially considering our countries were founded by immigrants usurping the natives that were here first. No, we can't take in everyone, but is this who we have become?

With the understanding that none of us are indigenous to the United States except for the Native Americans, this debate has me scratching and even shaking my head (no matter what Spicer says). We forgot the stories about how our ancestors came here and made a life that was different from their native lands. The vast majority of us are not from the United States of America. Have we forgotten? Has Trump forgotten? Surely not. Or is it deeper, the exercising of the inner racist he claims not to be? Does that NAACP definition of a racist—the intersection of racial prejudice and power—fit him?

What I wonder now is, what do we look like globally? How do other nations see us? Is that even important? Just a few months after Trump took office, the Pew Research Center reported that the president and many of his proposed policies were surprisingly unpopular with other countries, with only 22 percent of thirty-seven nations having confidence that Trump could properly manage international issues. This can be compared with Barack Obama's 64 percent confidence level when he left office. To be fair, there were two countries that viewed Trump more favorably than Obama—Israel and, of course, Russia.

If we look back on the United States' reputation over the last twenty years, other countries likely began to become concerned in 2000 when our country could not immediately determine who had won the presidency. It was between Al Gore and George W. Bush, and it took almost a month before a winner was declared, coming down to 537 votes in Florida. Not only were we dealing with all the confusion and conspiracy theories, but, of course, the world was watching. In the past, other countries were seen as often having unstable governments, but never the United States.

The fact that we could not immediately determine who our president would be did not look good for our reputation as a well-managed, all-powerful leader of the free world. We went from being seen as secure and stable to a practically rudderless nation that could not even accurately count votes. Until that point, for the most part we always felt that our way of choosing a leader was the most fair and accurate method. We were often shocked by how other countries struggled with inaccurate results, accusations of bribery, and even candidates that went missing before election day.

Then the 2000 election happened, and the United States was seen as being not only unorganized, but unable to fairly elect a president to the highest office in the land. They watched as we fought over "hanging, pregnant, and dimpled chads" and struggled with recounts and dealt with in-fighting. Even after George W. Bush was certified as the president, we were still struggling internally and our reputation among the other countries was severely diminished.

I was working at the White House then, after having covered the Clinton administration during its second term. Like the rest of the country, and the world, I was surprised by how fragile our electoral system seemed and how vulnerable it looked to us and everyone else. It was that sense of uncertainty that was the most difficult to come to terms with, especially for the people I was working hard to represent as I continued building my journalism career with AURN at the White House. It was, and still is, my goal to question and search for answers for minorities and others who are often marginalized and maligned and overlooked in our society while I cover the topics of the day as well.

During the Clinton administration, things were far from perfect, including the controversial crime bill, which disproportionately affected people of color. Nevertheless, the president did have a positive relationship with minority communities, particularly Black and Brown people. So, when the election results were unclear, we were all unsure of what we would have to endure, especially if the Bush administration took office. With Al Gore, it was safe to assume that there would be change, but not a total shift in domestic and international policy. If Bush took office, the Black community was concerned that rights would be scaled back.

As we contemplated that scenario, the world was likely doing the same thing. They knew, like it or not, what they were dealing with since Clinton had been in office for eight years. A Bush win meant uncertainly, and as we all know, that never instills confidence in people. A good example is the stock market, which is based largely on investor confidence. If people are feeling unsure for some reason, the stocks take a dive. When people are satisfied, the stocks climb.

That 2000 election was the world's first real peek at just how unpredictable the United States could be, and no one wanted unpredictability from the traditionally most stable nation in the world. The issue of close and contested election results, something we didn't think we'd have to deal with again after the Gore vs. Bush debacle, came back in full force in 2016. It was predicted that the Democratic candidate would win; therefore, it was assumed that change would not be extreme, with basic policies remaining, particularly internationally.

We all know what happened. Despite those polls and predictions, Trump was declared the winner in a tight race, winning the Electoral College, but losing the popular vote. Many people who went to sleep hoping for one result, awoke to a new reality that Donald Trump would be president of the United States. Internationally, the world was shocked—except for one Communist country—and almost immediately there was evidence of election results being influenced or outright hacked. The world was unprepared for this new leadership because no one had any idea how things would change. The same was probably true for the incoming administration since a surprisingly large number of key appointments had no political experience, thus no idea how to govern. Now we are finding that many cannot even pass the once-standard security clearance required to handle classified information.

The Trump election may not have been so impactful internationally if the 2000 debacle had not occurred. However, the United States now has a pattern, twice in sixteen years, of having challenges with our election process. That doesn't give other nations confidence that the United States will be able to handle something as complex as international relations when its election process seems so tenuous.

Of course, the election process was only one small brick in the wall of international issues that the Trump administration was constructing. Speaking of walls, naturally there was that physical wall that was threatened throughout the campaigning process and has continued to this day. How can we try to build and foster good relations with another country when we come out with threats of building a wall to clearly define our separation? It's not only the physical wall, but the fact that it represents that we (or more specifically, the Trump administration) does not care about building relations and working together.

This new policy of bullying and intimidation to get cooperation from other countries flies in the face of the history of the United States and how we deal with most of the other nations in the world. Traditionally, while we have had conflict with many other countries that even resulted in the use of aggression, trade embargoes, and even war, our reputation was that we, as a country, would work to foster good international relations, or seemingly so. If we weren't close allies, at least we usually worked to achieve mutual relationships based on give and take.

Trump's threats against Mexico during the campaign gave everyone a clear message that if he won the election, international relations would be forever impacted, and they have been. The only thing I can say is that he was clear from the start about where he stood and hasn't wavered. So that meant for better or worse, Mexico was put on notice during that campaign that if Trump won, things between the two countries would be different.

His most controversial idea has, of course, been the idea of "building a wall" between the two countries. The animosity was swift and immediate. Any time there's a need for a wall or border, it's a clear and physical symbol of the fact that the people on one side are not welcome on the other side. It's a constant reminder. Most of the world assumed that for the most part, especially among the most developed countries, an actual border was less necessary than solid immigration policies.

The Pew Research Center found that when it comes to building a wall along the U.S.-Mexico border, 76 percent of countries are opposed to the idea. Naturally, feelings are stronger in Mexico, where it is reported that nine out of ten oppose the building of a wall. The reason it is so divisive is not just the wall, but the way it was "proposed." It was largely used as a metaphor for Trump's overall leadership plan—to segregate, punish, and strong-arm any nation that did not agree with everything he proposed. Mexico was an easy target to use as an example of jobs going across the border where manufacturing and lower cost meant companies can lower expenses and thus increase profits, something you would think that Trump would support. That was not the case because he needed a whipping post, a country to use as a scapegoat. That scapegoat was Mexico.

In his rallies, Trump yelled that Mexico was taking our jobs and allowing their most dangerous citizens to cross the border into the United States. Talk of a wall was an easy way to show his supporters that first, he was taking a bold stand, and second, he had a simple solution. In a campaign, a complicated international policy would never drum up excitement and support, but the chant of "build that wall" was the prefect rallying cry. It symbolized everything that he and his base saw as "bad"—immigration, job outsourcing, and cooperation between countries.

His stand was that if elected, there would be only one way—his—with no negotiation. Of course, that was not realistic, strategic, or beneficial for the long term, but none of that mattered. It energized his base with a message that was easily understood. Immigration, bad. Wall, good.

Prior to Trump's administration, the United States and Mexico have had close economic and diplomatic ties, which made sense because we share a border. The fact is that Mexico has often been helpful to the United States, not only through trade but also in a humanitarian effort. The country denounced the horrible 9/11 attacks and even provided substantial support after the devastation of Hurricane Katrina. Today, the Pew Research study finds that 93 percent of Mexicans have no confidence in President Trump.

In response to Trump's assuming office, Enrique Pena Nieto, the Mexican president, cancelled his scheduled trip that had been planned prior to the 2016 election results. That was also following the executive order Trump signed in January about construction of the much-discussed wall. At the time of the final writing of this book, no actual money to construct a new "border wall" has been approved by Congress, and the issue has been discussed during the creation of the 2018 and 2019 U.S. budgets, despite vowing that Mexico would shoulder the financial burden of construction.

As I've learned from watching the changing of several administrations and how they transition power, it's all about the approach. Just like in the South, you can propose something that folks don't like if you present it in the right way or drop in a familiar phrase of "bless your heart." It is also kind of what we do in Baltimore; some folks will sweeten the words with "hon" (!) at the end of sentence. If a leader had legitimate concerns about border security, the effective approach would be to strategically consider long-term relations and work with the adjoining country to determine the best way to collectively improve security. But that wouldn't have made an effective campaign slogan, and it may be beyond the president's leadership capabilities, if we are being honest. Working in harmony with another country to get results that both countries can live with is a skill that not everyone possesses but one that every good president needs, from my observation.

In the lead up to the Trump presidential victory, there were things I remember well coming out of candidate Trump's mouth during his campaigning, like the term "Crooked Hillary." But more than any other words, I remember the call: "Who's gonna pay for the wall?" And the response from the crowd: "Mexico!" I think back to the campaign promises that couldn't be kept, like George H. W. Bush saying, "Read my lips—No new taxes!" That promise was a farce. It was the older brother to the unlikely 2016 promise that Mexico would pay for the wall. So ultimately, who's left holding the very pricey funding bag for this southern border wall? "Not I!" says Mexico. President Trump now says that Mexico will ultimately pay through the North American Free Trade Agreement (NAFTA).

What's especially interesting is that the southern border is not the only way Mexican immigrants can get into the United States. There's been concern about a NAFTA provision that was announced in 2015 that provides a way for long-haul truck drivers from Mexico to possibly smuggle people across the border. When NAFTA was signed in 1994, this Mexican truck effort was said to be a step toward economic integration among Mexico, the United States, and Canada. NAFTA also permits truckers from the United States and Canada to travel in and out of those countries as well.

Twenty-one years after NAFTA was signed in the Bill Clinton administration, the effort began with pilot programs that later became permanent. At least six Mexican trucking companies are allowed point-to-point hauling: from Mexico to one location in the United States. They are then allowed to return to Mexico with no stops in between. Critics have long been concerned about this NAFTA provision and the possibilities for smuggling illegals into the United States. So, if the fight is about cutting into the number of illegals, it may not be just about the wall.

Let me state for the record: I'm not accusing any of the trucking companies in the NAFTA agreement of smuggling people across the border. However, my point is that the whole thing isn't just about building a wall to prevent illegals from coming into this country. Truck smuggling is common and deadly. If we research the subject, there's a plethora of articles on smuggling undocumented persons using various methods. It's not just about the wall. It's about the overall issue and the differing parts of it that play into the problem.

NAFTA is about economics, but in the midst of the immigration debate with Mexico, there are concerns about worsening relations via the proposed border adjustment tax that would add more taxes on imported goods. CBC chairman Cedric Richmond says, "The border adjustment tax would hurt the country. Starting a trade war or harming relations with Mexico would harm this country. Not to mention we are supposed to be this great country that says give me your tired your poor or your huddled masses."

To the north, Canada has typically enjoyed a solid relationship with the United States, particularly during Democratic presidencies. The current administration couldn't be more different from Canada's prime minister Justin Trudeau on issues. Canada supports global trade and strong environmental policies, but the two did agree on the approval of the Keystone XL pipeline, which the Obama administration opposed. Trump and the United States have the lowest favorability ratings in Canada since 2002, with only 22 percent confidence in the president and 43 percent confidence in the country.

Trump has had a strained relationship with Germany's chancellor Angela Merkel, often of his own doing. Because Germany has Europe's largest economy, it makes good economic sense to manage workable relations. The March 2017 meeting between Trump and Merkel at the White House was overshadowed by his stand-offish body posture while she tried to engage him and obviously worked to establish a rapport, saying in the news conference that the two should speak to, not about, each other.

Her approach was one of diplomacy: "We held a conversation where we were trying to address also those areas where we disagree, but we tried to bring people together . . . tried to find a compromise that is good for both sides." During the press conference, Trump talked generally about nations needing to "pay their fair share" for the cost of defense and that many nations owe money to NATO and the United States (never mentioning Germany).

Then he made a bizarre comment: "As far as wiretapping, I guess this past administration, at least we have something in common perhaps." Merkel seemed to have no idea what he was talking about or why he was saying that to her. He was probably referring to the incident in 2013 when there was talk of the United States monitoring Germany's leaders' phone calls, but nothing was ever proven. At the time of these reports, President Obama offered his personal apologies to the German leader for what was alleged to have happened.

Back to the Trump and Merkel meeting. They also immediately disagreed on the topic of immigration, and Merkel indicated that basically they should agree to disagree. Later, Trump followed up the meeting with two tweets:

Despite what you have heard from the FAKE NEWS, I had a GREAT meeting with German Chancellor Angela Merkel. Nevertheless, Germany owes . . . 8:15 AM—Mar 18, 2017

Vast sums of money to NATO & the United States must be paid more for the powerful, and very expensive, defense it provides to Germany!—8:23 AM—Mar 18, 2017

The meeting began as awkwardly as it ended, when Trump wouldn't shake her hand as they posed for pictures. The photographers called for them to shake hands as they are accustomed to, often guiding photo subjects in standard photo-op situations. Merkel had to say to him, "Do you want to have a handshake?" To which Trump looked down at the floor.

Certainly, she was aware of his talk at his rallies, his rhetoric about the "catastrophic" immigration policy that Germany had adopted, and he also said that she had ruined the country. In addition, he mentioned that he was upset that she was the *Time* magazine Person of the Year in 2015. He thought that should have been . . . him. It was yet another example of Trump not being able to go beyond his personal feelings.

Previously, Germany did not have a positive view of the United States during the George W. Bush administration, and Bush became less popular with the Germans the longer he was in office. Then when Obama moved into the White House, German favorability ratings went up. Now they are back to where they were with Bush.

The United States and Britain have been allies throughout the twentieth century, up to 2016. Then came Trump. Britain had already gone through the Brexit situation, so they were somewhat in flux, which did not help matters. When Trump retweeted an anti-Muslim video from British extremists, that upset most of the country. Even Prime Minister Theresa May gave him a mild rebuke. Trump being Trump, he fired back on Twitter that she should concentrate on catching the terrorists that have plagued the country, obviously not a subject to be taken lightly or discussed on social media.

Typically, both countries have shared intelligence information and other strategic intents, and that relationship is probably damaged at this point. Despite calls in Parliament to cancel Trump's January 2018 trip, May declined to do so. However, the animosity among other officials and citizens in Britain clearly showed they did not want Trump to visit their country. They got their wish as he abruptly canceled his plans the month he was due to arrive. Speculation is that he did it because he knew there would be much more protest and bitterness than his preferred cheering crowds and rallies.

Many other nations have faced challenges with Trump, but none as much as North Korea and the threats that could affect the world. During the Clinton administration, relations were on the rise between the two countries, primarily due to the work of U.S. Secretary of State Madeleine Albright. Once Clinton left office and Bush came in, relations again turned sour, with North Korea performing its first nuclear test in 2006. They performed a second test in 2009 by launching a rocket, just after Barack Obama took office; however, it was unsuccessful. Until 2016, North Korea performed several long-range missile and nuclear tests, facing sanctions from the United Nations, including the United States.

Relations reached their most elevated level in 2017. First, North Korea performed yet another missile test, this one reportedly capable of reaching Alaska. Then instead of working to strengthen relations, Trump resorted to Twitter and referred to Kim Jong-un as "rocket man" and said that he was on "a suicide mission" for both himself and his entire country. That resulted in Kim Jong-un referring to Trump as "mentally deranged" and saying he would pay dearly for the threats he had lobbed their way. The North Korean leader's comments were not unexpected—after all he is a dictator—but having an American president who responds to military aggression with name calling is not only disappointing from a leadership perspective but it's also unproductive. What's the point? The final straw was when Trump tweeted:

> North Korean Leader Kim Jong Un just stated that the "Nuclear Button is on his desk at all times." Will someone from his depleted and food starved regime please inform him that I too have a Nuclear Button, but it is a much bigger & more powerful one than his, and my Button works!—7:49 PM—Jan 2, 2018

First of all, there is no actual nuclear button on his desk, and the size of it would make no difference as it relates to its power, so it made no sense. It was more needless aggression and posturing, harking back to locker room machismo and bragging about who has the larger penis and how that means they are somehow more powerful or successful. One thing that we all learned, when someone talks about something so much it usually means they are trying to compensate for a shortcoming. At least that's what I have always heard. For President Trump, size matters.

That leaves the elephant in the room, the country most important to Trump, sometimes seemingly more important than the United States—that is, of course, Russia. Trump and Russia go way back, and I can't even attempt to track all that they have done together. I mean, there was the Miss Universe competition in 2013, an unfruitful deal to build a Trump Tower in Moscow, and visits by family members during the campaign season. Then there were supposedly meetings with Trump campaign staffers and a proposal to improve United States and Russian relations if Trump won.

Along the way, there was email hacking of the Democratic campaign and meetings with Putin and the Russian ambassador in London. It was discovered that Trump campaign aide George Papadopoulos was meeting with the Kremlin, looking for "dirt" on Hillary Clinton and lying about it to the FBI. Many reporter emails were captured in that Wikileaks drama. My emails made it into the ugly scenario. All reporters emailed both sides to get information. The only problem—no one knows what the emails looked like in the Trump camp because they were not hacked. I sent emails to them as well. Then there were records showing Donald Trump Jr. and Jared Kushner meeting with Russians. Then during the campaign, Trump continued to distance himself, denying any real connection with Russia and their involvement in social media "bots" and false stories created to incite American voters.

All of this would not matter if it weren't for the interference in the election that everyone fears. How, as a country, has our election process become so fragile that it can be manipulated by a foreign government? In October 2016, U.S. intelligence agencies indicated their consensus that the Russian government had interfered with the election. Before he left office, Obama ordered a review of the U.S. election results, but Trump dismissed the CIA's report that the Russians had been involved. Trump and the campaign's involvement with Russia is now being investigated. On March 28, 2017, I did my best to get answers at a press conference, which was presided over by Sean Spicer. All I wanted to know was how would this White House two months in work to change its image over Russia? Well the world shifted on that question. Here's how!

MR. SPICER: April, go ahead.

Q: All right, thank you. Sean—don't seem so happy. Anyway, with all of these investigations, questions of what is is, how does this administration try to revamp its image? Two-and-a-half months in, you've got this Yates story today, you've got other things going on, you've got Russia, you've got wiretapping, you've got—

MR. SPICER: No, we don't have that.

Q: There are investigations on Capitol Hill—

MR. SPICER: No, no—I get it. But you keep—I've said it from the day that I got here until whatever that there is no connection. You've got Russia. If the President puts Russian salad dressing on his salad tonight, somehow that's a Russian connection. But every single person—

Q: It's beyond that. You're making it—

MR. SPICER: Well, no—I appreciate your agenda here, but the reality is—

Q: It's not my agenda.

MR. SPICER: No, hold on. At some point, report the facts. The facts are that every single person who has been briefed on this subject has come away with the same conclusion—Republican, Democrat. So I'm sorry that that disgusts you. You're shaking your head. I appreciate it, but—

Q: I'm shaking my head and I'm listening, and I'm trying to get—

MR. SPICER: Okay, but understand this—that at some point, the facts are what they are, and every single person who has been briefed on this situation with respect to the situation with Russia—Republican, Democrat, Obama-appointee, career—have all come to the same conclusion. At some point, April, you're going to have to take "no" for an answer, with respect to whether or not there was collusion.

Q: But my question was how do you change the perception of—

MR. SPICER: We're going to keep doing everything we're doing to make sure that the president—that what the president told the American people he was going to do to fulfill those pledges and promises that he made, to bring back jobs, to grow the economy, to keep our nation safe—that's what he's been focused on since day one. We're going to keep focusing on that every single day.

Q: But when Condi Rice comes Friday. Condi Rice did not support this president. She did not go to the convention. She comes—what is on the agenda, and how is their relationship? Has it healed since 2006 when he used a very negative word to describe her?

MR. SPICER: So, here's what I'll—hey, it's interesting that you ask those two questions back to back. On the one hand, you're saying what are we doing to improve our image, and then here he is, once again, meeting somebody that hasn't been a big supporter of his.

Q: But he called her that negative name in 2006.

MR. SPICER: No, no, but you put it—April, hold on. It seems like you're hell-bent on trying to make sure that whatever image you want to tell about this White House stays, because at the end of the day—

Q: I am just reporting what—

MR. SPICER: Okay, but you know what? You're asking me a question, and I'm going to answer it, which is the President— I'm sorry. Please stop shaking your head again. But at some point, the reality is that this president continues to reach out to individuals who've supported him, who didn't support him—Republicans, Democrats—to try to bring the country together and move forward on an agenda that's going to help every American. That's it, plain and simple. So if you're asking what we're doing, I think we continue to do it, which is to bring groups together that have been supportive of him, that haven't been supportive of him, but that to share a goal, which is finding common ground on areas of national security, of personal security, of economic security, of job creation, of safer communities, of education, of healthcare that can unite us as a country and make the country stronger.

None of this is meant as a criticism of the president, but a question of the reality as national leaders had been caught on camera giving the new president the side-eye, or with facial expressions of confusion about what he is saying or doing. By all accounts, it seems that our international standing has been diminished. Too many examples within a little over a year have caused Europe to say they must go it alone without the United States after the decision to leave the Paris agreement on climate change.

Jeh Charles Johnson, who served as head of the Department of Homeland Security in the Obama administration, says, "Traditionally and historically when the United States finds itself in a tense international situation with a belligerent actor, the world counts on the United States to be the grown-up and ratchet down the temperature. It is hard for me to imagine as de-escalation occurs between us and North Korea when you have our president bragging about how his button is bigger than Kim Jung-un's button. I am very concerned about that. That is what most worries me on a global perspective."

NAACP president Cornell Brooks observes,

As a matter of rhetoric and reality, President Trump has advocated an immigration policy that has endeared him to both the hard right and white supremacist alt-right. In fact, President Trump's immigration policy is the discriminatory descendant of the Immigration Act of 1924, which used racist and anti-Semitic quotas to limit Jewish, Asian immigrants—as well as those from southern Europe. Lest any American or DREAMer miss the bigoted purpose and point of the Trump immigration goals, the President has argued for an end to chain migration or family reunification which disproportionately affects immigrant communities of color; adoption of a merit-based system which he suggested would favor immigrants from Norway while limiting those from 'shithole countries'; and reducing legal immigration by half, which would also have a racially disparate impact. One the president's most influential voices on immigration reform is none other than Attorney General Jeff Sessions who has offered unabashed praise for the Immigration Act. Presumably the President and Attorney General know that the Act was conceived during one of the most xenophobic periods in American history in which the Klan grew from a relative handful to two million members—inspired by this same anti-immigrant sentiment now inciting a rising hate crime rate in 2018. Not only is the Trump immigration policy the biased descendant of the Immigration Act, the anti-Muslim travel ban is the bigoted sibling of his equally biased immigration policy.

My question is, will this president pick up the torch where it was left off and travel to the continent of Africa to focus on trade, counterterrorism, and health issues? He has met with the head of the African Union, who denounced him for the shithole comment. However, does the term *shithole* reflect more of what Trump really thinks than giving these countries a helping hand? I spoke to many who are still unhappy about the direction our country has taken, domestically and internationally. To complicate matters, it has been reported by Reuters and others that Israel sent out deportation notices to thousands of African migrants that they have to either leave the country or go to jail. Reportedly, they are being offered money and a plane ticket, which has been met with a backlash in that country, one that once offered sanctuary to Jews. Remember Israel is one of only two counties whose approval of the United States has increased since Trump took office . . . you know, the other country. So, what I want to know is, are these countries feeling emboldened or justified in their new policy of removing or jailing immigrants instead of creating a path to citizenship? Are they mimicking the way the Trump administration is handling immigration? Is he setting a bad example for the world?

I worked on election night. but I also watched social media and called a friend, Republican Chris Darden, who is Black, for an interview for American Urban Radio Networks. Darden was a prosecutor in the O. J. Simpson trial. I talked with him about Donald Trump's election, and Darden was clear as to what he thought. Darden said, "I can't imagine why any good Republican would vote for Donald Trump given his positions on race, and sexism, his lack of competence, his lack of knowledge, his lack of any plans for the nation, his lack of understanding of how government works and how things are accomplished. And now look what has happened, we have given the village idiot the keys to the kingdom along with the House and Senate and the ability to appoint the next three Supreme Court Justices."

Darden offered something else, this time about resistance, saying, "People have to be ready for a new era of activism. Getting involved in your local community and politics and making your voice heard is very important because we don't have a dog in this hunt anymore. We are for the most part in this part, we the minorities. And it is clearer that we are the minorities than ever because we don't have any branch of government and none of it belongs to us anymore. There is going to be a conservative or close to a conservative Supreme Court. They are going to have the House, they are going to have the Senate, they are going to have the White House and we are going to have to assert ourselves and assert our agenda."

That assertion was on the mind of activist and entertainer Harry Belafonte in the time between the election and the January 20, 2017, inauguration. Mr. Belafonte, in his New York apartment, offered his take on this democratic transition, noting that a large swath of the nation was not happy about those people I describe as being in the fetal position for weeks. To be honest, many still are and are searching for hope of a better day after the anomaly at the polls—the second time in less than twenty years that the person with the most votes did not win, just like in 2000, when the U.S. Supreme Court decided who the president would be.

On this current political crisis, Belafonte offered something from W. E. B. Du Bois, who told him decades ago, "True liberation will come for Black people when things in America get more painful." Belafonte talked of how President-elect Donald Trump would "blur the lines," and with the great pain would come a dis-ease that would cause radical activism that effectuates change. Belafonte, one of the fathers of the Woman's March the day after the inauguration, was hopeful for more activism, but he is not seeing the persistence and consistency of the protests of today like there were in days past.

So, our problems are not only domestic but international as well. As Cedrick Richmond noted, "Other countries are not just shaking their heads at Trump anymore, they are shaking their heads at the United States of America." In writing this book, I talked to a major European representative who said that Trump is such a disruptor that leaders of other countries don't know what to make of him. The world is looking at this and how it could upset democracy because some people are choosing not to believe what the media is telling them anymore. They don't want the truth, and that has been the recipe for chaos in other countries.

In addition, Congressman Adam Schiff (D-CA) said, "President Trump has seriously damaged our standing in the world to the detriment of our national security and global stability. He has cozied up to dictators, called core components of the international order like NATO 'obsolete,' and withdrawn from the Paris Climate Accords. Beyond these destructive words and actions, his attacks on the free press give succor to authoritarian leaders around the world, undermining decades of efforts to spread democratic values and human rights."

Is there an effort for a national racial cleansing of the United States, as Michael Steele suggests, in an effort to control the browning of the nation? Some think so, particularly with the focus on Mexico (not Canada), Muslims, and others in the Middle East. The Israel policy has Africans march in the streets of Jerusalem, with signs to include one that read "Do Black Lives Matter in Israel?" This is eerily familiar to what is happening in the United States. Where are the Black and Brown people supposed to go? And who makes that decision?

It's my job to keep asking those questions.

· 9 ·

Women at Work

The year 2017 was supposed to be the "Year of the Woman." It was touted everywhere, bolstered by the polls that assured us Hillary Clinton would be the next president. It turned out not to be the year of the woman the way we expected, but it did so in other ways. The Women's March on Washington, held the day after the Trump inauguration and led primarily by women, started a movement of women becoming more visible and more vocal about their treatment at work and in society. In that march, and the hundreds of others that occurred around the country, there were pink hats and bold slogans. The march was in-your-face and aggressive, showing that women could be just as assertive as men.

Then came the #MeToo movement, started by actresses who had been harassed—physically, sexually, and emotionally—by men in power. The interesting part of that for me was that the harassment was found to manifest itself not only in professional challenges but also in emotional and physical issues for those who had been subject to that behavior in the workplace.

In another amazing example of the power of women, particularly Black women, on December 12, 2017, polling showed that Roy Moore was defeated in the contentious Alabama Senate race, primarily due to the turnout of women of color. There were viral videos of women dancing as they left the polls, bolstered by the fact that they were showing up and pulling together to make a real difference in their own community, a difference that would affect the entire country. Theirs was a stand for the moral high ground. The irony is that a stand like this would not have been tolerated more than fifty years ago, when African

165

Americans marched for voting rights in Selma, Alabama. Today, Selma looks like a town that time forgot, yet it was so pivotal in our history. That march, known as the Bloody Sunday March, was key in getting Congress to pass the Voting Rights Act. Back then, and in 2017, the Black Belt region, a region called that because of its rich soil, made the difference. I consider that region rich in spirit as well.

This job I have been blessed to have has made it quite clear that the spirit of resilience is there in the worst of times. Also, more importantly, you can't write off folks. Everyone has a story, and their stories will be told one way or another.

I guess I fall in that category as someone who never thought of her own personal story. It has taken tearful women I have met on this journey to force me to understand that although I am not the story, I have helped them or shaped their story in one way or another. The memes and viral videos are more than amusement for those going through something that I am not always privy to. I have been in shock and even numbed by some of the darts I have taken. I am only human. I am not a superwoman, although it may sometimes seem like I am.

I knew that everything I had been through over the last couple of years was taking a toll on my health, but I wasn't sure why. Then I saw a report published by Catalyst, a global nonprofit founded in 1962 that works with corporations to improve working conditions for women. The article really resonated with me because of the way I have had to fend off attacks and deal with unnecessary aggression as I try to do my job. The report released in February 2018 is called "Day-to-Day Experiences of Emotional Tax among Women and Men of Color in the Workplace." It found that "a majority of women of color—specifically individuals who identify with Asian, Black, Latino, and multiracial backgrounds—experience an 'Emotional Tax' in US workplaces affecting overall health, well-being and ability to thrive." Emotional tax takes place when "there is an undue burden levied on women of color because of exclusionary behaviors, affecting their overall health and well-being as well as making them feel constantly on guard."

It felt good to learn that what I was going through, the toll it had taken on my health, was a real problem, especially for Black women. The article also said that "women of color are in a constant state of being 'on guard' because of their gender, race and/or ethnicity."

On guard is the polite term because my head is on the swivel every day, not knowing when the next shoe will drop. All this, not to mention the death threats. Think of being concerned for your family's safety as well as your own, and the very people you go to for help with this—the White House Correspondents' Association (WHCA) that I am member of—says, "We are not law enforcement, and anyway you get called on by the press secretary and you are on CNN." One person in that illustrious group made that comment. I chalk it up to his ignorance.

The WHCA board is working with groups to chronicle the hate that is festering as a result of those screaming "fake news," but what I wanted was for the group to express to the White House that this must stop. When I got that response from a man who typically doesn't like to rock the boat, I was floored. What a jerk. I wish I had never told him about my concerns, and I know I would never vote for him to be on that board again. The president of the WHCA took up my cause, but to hear someone say that . . . !

The stress I've had to endure after the personal and professional attacks by Trump and his White House have been mentally taxing and have made me actually feel sick more often than I ever have before. Other Black women who have experienced the wrath of Trump have had similar experiences, including Susan Rice, Maxine Waters, and Frederica Wilson.

Dnika J. Travis, PhD, vice president of research at Catalyst, says, "Over time, these daily battles take a heavy toll on women of color, creating a damaging link between their health and the workplace. And because of consequences associated with Emotional Tax, companies must begin to take intentional action to avoid possible harm to their businesses and employees' health and well-being."

The report notes that women of color feel on guard "when they have to outwork and outperform their colleagues." That pertains to me because being a woman and a minority in what used to be a White male–dominated profession, in the Trump era where the perception is women don't rank, has its own challenges. And when you pile on harassment and abuse, it takes it to a whole different level.

The Catalyst report was a follow-up to a previous study called "Emotional Tax: How Black Women and Men Pay More at Work and How Leaders Can Take Action" by Dnika J. Travis, Jennifer Thorpe-Moscon, and Courtney McCluney. That study, which also appeared in

Essence magazine, found that emotional tax may impair the health and success of Black women and men.

I wrote this book in part so that people would have a better understanding of my beat. People wonder why I bring up questions of race and why I am persistent when trying to get answers. This is why: the Black community faces so many challenges that other people are not aware of. I believe that it's part of my responsibility to bring these challenges to light, and hopefully there will eventually be change.

So, 2017 might not have been the year of the woman the way we expected, but the Trump White House did give women, especially minority women, the motivation to become more vocal about the challenges we face. It also reminded us that while we can be aggressive and persistent when necessary, we also need to be aware of its toll on our health.

It has been quite chaotic since Trump took office. In the many years I have been working my assignment at the White House, it has never looked or felt like this. I am not that girl who began covering this prestigious beat in 1997 anymore. I am no longer wide-eyed and eager for the experience. After what I have just been through, I have become more cautious, jaded, and suspicious, always waiting for what's to come next.

At the beginning of my career, I would have never imagined that I would be making the news. People often say, "reporters shouldn't be the story," and I agree. I hate being the news. It's not like any of it has been planned. It is all the result of an aggressive and defensive administration that is reluctant to provide any real information. They have lashed out at me, and that has made the news. It's not usually my response that is in question; it is what I have had to endure.

In all this turmoil, I have had to reassure myself at times. You know that you have yourself. It's okay to admit it. I do it too. I have to, in order to keep up with what is going on and what is being said about me and keep it all in perspective. I also need to make sure I'm not being quoted as saying something that I did not say. It's my reputation, and I have to protect it at all costs.

In 2016, I would have never imagined that if I did an Internet search on myself I would see such a diverse list of articles. Here are just a few of the headlines, and it's interesting how they play up each event. I know the folks publishing these articles use the most graphic descriptors possible to get eyeballs on their pages, but I do find it interesting. Here are some of the headlines I found and my responses:

- April Ryan Asks Political Questions No One Else Will—*That is true, and I always will.*
- April Ryan: I've Received Death Threats—*That is an unfortunate reality in this political climate.*
- April Ryan, Sarah Sanders Have Tense Face Off over Porter—*I wouldn't refer to that as a "tense face off"; she did try to avoid my questions and I kept asking, but I was not tense at all!*
- HUD Staffer Apologizes for Calling Reporter "Miss Piggy"—*As she should have.*
- April Ryan Says Journalists Have Police "On Speed Dial" for Threats—*This is yet another reality, and something I never thought I'd have to say.*
- White House Reporter April Ryan and Trump Aide Omarosa Manigault Used to Be Friends. Now Their Feud Is at Epic Levels—*I know people love a good "catfight" as they like to call it, but this wasn't really a feud, more of me realizing I couldn't be friends with her any longer because of her dangerous lies, but I understand why they used that term.*
- April Ryan Slammed on Twitter for Gushing over Oprah Winfrey: "Shame on You"—*Well, this is from Fox News, and I don't know that I gushed or that I was slammed for what I tweeted, but I do think it is great that a Black woman of her caliber is even thought of as a candidate. Here's my tweet, you decide:*

If @Oprah ran for president in 2020, she is every person. She has been poor & now rich. She is also a self-made billionaire. She has a grasp of the issues as she used to cover local politics. She can articulate any issue and she has mass appeal beyond race & gender. 2:17 PM—Jan 8, 2018

I think you get my point. Just like the title of this book, I have been under fire, and those are the tame stories. As you can imagine, it gets much worse, but I can't allow myself to go down that road. There's really no need to put myself through that since I've already lived through it.

These past two years have even amazed me as I have come to have a clearer understanding of what it means to stand for something in the middle of a storm. There is one thing I figured out along the way. Standing up for yourself is really not that hard, especially when you put it into context. However, what has happened on the job is a lot easier than other situations in my life. It is nothing compared to losing my mother after trying to "will her to live" in her last six months of life. It is nothing compared to having meaningful family relationships that are so complex that love is all you have. What has happened is nothing compared to growing up Baltimore Strong. It is nothing compared to raising two daughters essentially by myself since their birth into their teens and young womanhood.

Maybe people thought I would be weaker, that I would give in, but that's not how I was raised. My mother always said "never give up." In this case, I take her words as "never give in." When I face adversity, I come back strong. It might slow me down for a minute, I might have to catch my breath, but then I'm back at it and there's no stopping me. That's where I am now. I do not have time for people trying to use their words to insult me or getting aggressive so that I won't have a follow-up question. While I might not feel comfortable being in the news, I'm very comfortable with how I conduct myself on the job.

With all this under my belt, I am still blessed and honored to cover the White House daily and be considered an esteemed veteran at this job. Make no mistake about it, I have the greatest respect for the office of the president and the president himself. My respect for the office runs deep. It is more about those who are in the inner sanctum of the White House who have disdain for me. I understand that people are making the attacks, not the institution of the presidency.

However, I still have faith in this country and the people of this great land. I am the example they want to set for the White House press corps. The administration's attack is not just on me, but the entire press. This is not a test, but the real thing, a challenge, and we will see if their attack is successful in the November 2018 midterm elections. For me, I plan to stay on the job, continuing to ask about all of America, especially Black America, because unfortunately the community does not get a fair shake. If the neo-Nazis and alt-right are upset, there's nothing I can do about that. I was there before they even thought of a man like Donald Trump for president. Who are we as a people if we can't allow for a difference of views and opinions without being in danger of physical harm, especially if I do not look like you or speak like you? Individual differences and opposing thought is what has made this country great. Yes, I said it. This country is great and has always been, but do we have blemishes, flaws, and warts? Oh, yes. Do we deal with them? Yes!

I report daily in protest—my job, which I have always enjoyed, is now my form of protest, my marching, and even my "taking a knee" for other journalists of all races and genders. The protest is in the form of coming to work daily, asking questions, being professional, and not giving in to the taunts and sneers from the White House and other like-minded Trump minions. My protest is in your face, showing I am not dissuaded by the name-calling or minor juvenile attempts to hurt me. I am not thrown by attempts to offer career-ending lies about me. I have receipts to prove otherwise.

Previously, I never viewed my reporting as a form of protest but as something I was trained to do and continue to do until I choose to leave. It is my right to report and ask questions. But now this reporting has taken on a new meaning. My protest is active and goes against those who offer racist remarks as I continue to ask the same questions I have asked since day one. My protest is not silent. It puts that glaring spotlight on issues that would normally be swept under the rug. My protest is meant to offer truth and unbiased questioning. People always ask how I do it, how I go back.

It's simple. My truth is difficult, it's not easy, but it is empowering for me. I hope it is for you as well.

Index

About the Author

April Ryan has been a White House correspondent for the American Urban Radio Networks since the Clinton administration. In addition, she can be seen almost daily as a political analyst for CNN. She has been featured in *Vogue, Cosmopolitan,* and *Elle* magazines as well as the *New York Times, Washington Post,* and *Politico,* to name a few, and has appeared on *The Late Show with Stephen Colbert, Anderson Cooper 360, Hardball, Meet the Press,* and many other television news programs. She is the 2017 National Association of Black Journalists Journalist of the Year. Ryan resides in Baltimore, Maryland.